No Ways Tired

A volume in
Research, Advocacy, Collaboration, and Empowerment Mentoring Series
Donna Ford, *Series Editor*

No Ways Tired

The Journey for Professionals of Color in Student Affairs

Volume I
Change Is Gonna Come:
New and Entry-Level Professionals

edited by

Monica Galloway Burke
Western Kentucky University

U. Monique Robinson
Vanderbilt University

INFORMATION AGE PUBLISHING, INC.
Charlotte, NC • www.infoagepub.com

Library of Congress Cataloging-in-Publication Data

A CIP record for this book is available from the Library of Congress
http://www.loc.gov

ISBN: 978-1-64113-757-7 (Paperback)
       978-1-64113-758-4 (Hardcover)
       978-1-64113-759-1 (ebook)

CONTENTS

FOREWORD

I will never forget the day when I first met Rev. Dr. James Edward Cleveland at the Gospel Music Workshop of America—affectionately known as "GMWA." Visiting the workshop as a kid, alongside several adult members of my home church, New Hope Church of God in Christ (COGIC), it would be years before I fully appreciated the impact of that single experience on my own lifetime development as a preacher, teacher, musician, and "foot soldier" for racial and social justice. Almost a foreshadowing of how my own identities would evolve and meld over the course of my life, I was mesmerized watching the "King of Gospel" simultaneously command dozens in the music pit about tempo, while directing hundreds in the choir on pitch and diction, yet never losing focus in orating to thousands in the audience about the power (*dunnamis* in Greek) that lies within us to "do what we got to do in this journey called life," Cleveland said as best I can remember. With the band in full effect, choir in perfect harmony, and audience standing on their feet in thunderous applause, Rev. Cleveland burst into solo: "I don't feel noways tired . . . come too far from where I, I, I [repeated] started from. . . ." It was over—cheers, tears, and hugs everywhere.

Fast forward a dozen years or so. Now a music double-major (along with religious studies) at the University of Virginia, I was asked to declare at least two musical genres as sites of primary study and performance focus. Reminiscent of my first exposure to Rev. James Cleveland and the GMWA, I chose ethnomusicology as a way to connect with gospel, jazz, blues, and other Afrocentric artforms. Pretty soon, I was reading books about James Weldon Johnson composing the Black National Anthem. I spent long hours

No Ways Tired, pages vii–x
Copyright © 2019 by Information Age Publishing
All rights of reproduction in any form reserved.

in sound booths in Old Cabell Hall, listening to recordings of Aretha Franklin's "Respect" to trace its epistemic gospel roots. And, believe it or not, I burned the midnight oil in the basement of the music library on weekends, writing expository essays about homiletical musicality—that is, the rhythmic moment central to most Black preaching styles where the preacher and listener (congregation) join forces in a self-orchestrated, call-and-response experience that not only brings the sermon (or homily) to an end, but can also bring the "dull, tired, and asleep" to their feet in reverent applause.

My senior research project sprung from this curiosity—what is this musical moment in Black preaching? What stimulates the chemistry of this seemingly organic action-reaction in church settings? And, what does it do for all those involved in it? I would watch videos of famous preachers like Bishop TD Jakes, Bishop Gilbert Earl Patterson (now deceased), Dr. James Cone (now deceased), Rev. James Cleveland, and the late Bishop Charles Harrison Mason, Founder of the COGIC, to identify and trace patterns and trends in the words, phrases, or actions that precipitated this shift from speaking to singing, standing, and shouting. In one project, I analyzed short clips of "gospel greats" like Twinkie Clark of "The Clark Sisters" playing riffs on a Hammond B-3 organ while squalling out in perfect rhythm with the audience:

> **Clark:** Let me do one thing before I leave the organ...
> **Audience:** C'mon Twinkie...do that thing.
> **Clark:** I want you to find somebody that look a little depressed...find somebody that look tired...find somebody that look lonely [sic].
> **Audience:** Talk, Twink!
> **Clark:** They just need somebody to hold them and tell 'em that they love 'em. Did you find somebody that look like they been going through?
> **Audience:** Yes!!! (cheers)
> **Clark:** Grab 'em and tell them this...for all you've been through God's got a blessing for ya [sic].

What I learned from my empirical work on Black preaching and musicality about this involuntary phenomenon is this: It is all but automatic, random, or unexpected. Though it appears to rise out of nowhere, it is the result of a far more complicated and *conscious* pattern of communication between the preacher (speaker) and the listener (audience) where the spoken word (what one says) connects with and reflects powerfully the frank realities of one's lived experience (what one has seen/done in the past) that it compels a behavioral response in the present. This instinctive form of communication reverbs from the scripture to the song, from the pulpit to the door, from the preacher to the believer, from the speaker to the listener, from the author to the reader, and *all souls* are lifted. It's when the communicator—whether preacher, speaker, or author—operates as both *educator* and *fighter*—conveying an authentic understanding of the daily struggles and social miseries that shape one's "earthly journey," but does so in a way that attaches difficulty to destiny, problems to payoff, trial to triumph, and weariness to well-doing as the Apostle Paul did in Galatians 6:9.

> And let us not be weary in well-doing: for in due season we shall reap, if we faint not. (KJV)

That is what Rev. James Cleveland did in so many of his gospel hits—he connected the music and message in ways that awaken, enliven, and inspire listeners to keep moving. He made gospel music and expression part of the salvation message. That's what he was doing when he penned the words to this famous gospel standard—he was teaching us and inspiring us all at once:

> I don't feel noways tired,
> I've come too far from where I started from.
> Nobody told me that the road would be easy,
> I don't believe He brought me this far to leave me.

And in that same tradition, *No Ways Tired: The Journey for Professionals of Color in Student Affairs* represents an invaluable gift to the universal library from which we draw knowledge, understanding, and insights. This book brings together over 70 student affairs professionals, scholar-practitioners, researchers, and thought leaders who represent some of the front-line fighters for social justice and equity in campuses and communities across the nation. Collectively, they represent hundreds of years of professional experience, thousands of hours of training, dozens of ethnic identities, languages, religions, and worldviews, yet a single focus unites them: Speaking truth to power about the *real* journey for professionals of color in student affairs.

This remarkable work is organized into three volumes and approximately 50 different chapters. Some authors, like Harold Brown, use scholarly narratives about his time in graduate school to name critical aspects of the journey for first-generation student affairs professionals of color—code switching, family ties, and social hostility. Others like Hoa Dieu Bui draw on that same courage to call out resistant cultures, dismissive messaging, and the problem of erasure. Where some books on student affairs professionals synthesize findings from empirical survey studies littered by statistics, bar graphs, and projections, *No Ways Tired* takes a fundamentally different approach casting experiential knowledge as a legitimate *way of knowing* and telling.

Through the intentional incorporation of stories, vignettes, anecdotes, poetry, and testimonios, the editors of this *truth tomb* make clear that (our) stories matter . . . so too do our lives, even in higher education and student affairs. Readers will be struck by the book's comprehensiveness and clarity, in my opinion. The book not only breaks new ground on the excavation of minority professionals' journey, but it crosses disciplinary silos and method-ological boundaries in a way that few competing titles do. *No Ways Tired* is at once biography and ethnography, history and philosophy, scholarship and opinion, even theory and practice . . . but it's certainly *not* just another book about people of color in student affairs.

This written gift is a formidable collection that chronicles and docu-ments the journeys of *real-life* professionals of color in student affairs, a pro-fessional field that prides itself on principles of belonging, equity, inclusion, justice, and love but knowingly has a long, long way to go to live out the true meaning of its creed when it comes to faculty and staff who live (and work) at the margin . . . or are pushed there forcefully either by those naturally endowed the power and privilege to do so or by institutional forces that sys-tematically demonize, diminish, discredit, or conspire to destroy conscious, courageous spirits of color journeying through the world of work to create revolutionary change *in the earth.*

To all those implied or named—my committed, courageous, *called* broth-ers and sisters across the globe within any and all axis of social difference—I offer this endorsement as encouragement:

> *We can't feel noways tired.* We might *get* tired some days but we must resist the urge to *be* tired. We can't stay in that state.
>
> *We've come too far from where we've started from.* Think about it. Some of us from modest upbringings, single-parent (but proud) homes, poorly resourced schools or unsafe neighborhoods or countries, through hostile graduate programs and foreign policies but yet we made it. That's the story of resilience. That's the power we have.
>
> *No, our road may not be easy,* but it will be worth it. You are enough. You belong here (in student affairs). You're actually here on *purpose.* And we need you to stay.
>
> *I don't believe we were brought this far to be left out or behind.* Read on and gain strength. Read on and be affirmed. Read on and find com-munity. Read on and nod in agreement. Read on and speak your truth. Whatever you do, read on.

—Terrell L. Strayhorn, PhD

INTRODUCTION

NO WAYS TIRED

The Journey for Professionals of Color in Student Affairs

Focusing on issues and perceptions of student affairs professionals of color is necessary for their recruitment, retention, and achievement. By sharing their visions of success, lessons learned, and cautionary tales, the insights offered by the chapters' authors can assist other professionals of color who are new and entry-level professionals in laying a path for their success and finding ways they can construct opportunities to flourish and thrive. Their stories highlight topics that need to be openly discussed in student affairs, such as marginalization, multiple identities, intersectionality, meritocracy, privilege, social capital, discrimination, and racism. Critical conversations about the experiences of professionals of color in student affairs must occur to make the profession and discipline of student affairs better and more responsive to professionals of color. As bell hooks (1989) asserted, "When we end our silence, when we speak in a liberated voice, our words connect us with anyone anywhere who lives in silence" (p. 18). The ultimate goal for *No Ways Tired* is to provide a space for silenced or ignored voices and to promote discussions regarding how higher education institutions can be more proactive in supporting and creating environments that are conducive to the success of professionals of color navigating their higher education careers.

Even though diversity is currently conveyed as a ubiquitous principle within institutions of higher education (Brayboy, 2003; Kayes, 2006), professionals of color still face such issues as discrimination (Phillips, 2002), the glass ceiling (Cornelius, 2002; Mong & Roscigno, 2010), and a lack of mentoring and access to networks (Brooks & Clunis, 2007; Burke & Carter, 2015; Palmer & Johnson-Bailey, 2005). Building a diverse staff is important, but institutions must then consider how to retain them and respond to their unique and culture-based needs (Cornelius, 2002; Pascarella & Terenzini, 1991). Organizations that value diversity in all forms have employees with higher job satisfaction, which promotes higher levels of productivity, retention, and increased revenue (Carnevale & Stone, 1994). Students also benefit when the student affairs staff is composed of people from various backgrounds (Flowers & Pascarella, 1999). However, for institutions to address the issues student affairs professionals of color face while supporting them, they must first acknowledge that problems exist. Since White individuals often see race as less of a problem than people of color do and typically have a very different perception of workplace diversity issues and climate (Harper & Hurtado, 2007), any efforts to address race-based issues can be challenging—and they must be addressed in proactive ways.

Although the literature is extensive on the retention of students and faculty of color in higher education, literature on the retention of higher education professionals of color is limited. This book endeavors to address this gap in literature. The narratives in this book can provide a lens for higher education institutions to develop strategies and initiatives to recruit, support, and retain student affairs professionals of color.

The work is divided into three volumes: entry-level, mid-level, and senior-level. In this volume, the authors have less than five years of experience in the student affairs field. It is our hope that readers will resonate with and understand the authors' perspectives and stories. We believe their collective voices illuminate the trials and tribulations that student affairs professionals of color experience. Their collective voices emphasize the tenacity and strength with which many student affairs professionals of color possess to effectively do their jobs and fulfill their purposes. The stories and strategies they share provide a resounding compass pointing north toward success and contentment, leading the way for those who come behind them. Predominately White institutions' (PWI) administrators and boards of trust must take time to read this book and *believe* the stories and, then, review their policies, procedures and cultural climate using the new lens they develop from these chapters; and also examine themselves to transform campus environments at all levels so that student affairs professionals of color feel supported and thrive.

We appreciate all the authors who shared their stories and most of all, Dr. Donna Y. Ford for providing us this tremendous opportunity. Her incredible drive and contagious vision inspired us.

The 20-year friendship shared by the co-editors exemplifies professional and personal support, mentoring, and love. This endeavor was an inspiring *labor* of love. We hope you enjoy and are inspired as well.

—**Monica Galloway Burke**
U. Monique Robinson

REFERENCES

Brayboy, B. M. J. (2003). The implementation of diversity in predominantly White colleges and universities. *Journal of Black Studies, 34*(1), 72–86.

Brooks, A. K., & Clunis, T. (2007). Where to now? Race and ethnicity in workplace learning and development research: 1980–2005. *Human Resource Development Quarterly, 18,* 229– 251.

Burke, M.G., & Carter, J. D. (2015) Examining perceptions of networking among African American women in student affairs. *NASPA Journal About Women in Higher Education, 8*(2), 140–155.

Carnevale, A. P., & Stone, S. C. (1994). Diversity beyond the golden rule. *Training and Development, 48*(10), 22–39.

Cornelius, N. (2002). *Building workplace equality: Ethics, diversity and inclusion.* London, England: Thomson.

Flowers, L.A., & Pascarella, E.T. (1999). Does college racial composition influence the openness to diversity of African American students? *Journal of College Student Development, 40*(6), 377–389.

Harper, S. R., & Hurtado, S. (2007). Nine themes in campus racial climates and implications for institutional transformation. In S. R. Harper, & L. D. Patton (Eds.), *Responding to the realities of race on campus. New Directions for Student Services* (No. 120, pp. 7–24). San Francisco, CA: Jossey-Bass.

hooks, b. (1989). *Talking back: Thinking feminist, thinking Black.* Boston, MA: South End Press.

Kayes, P. (2006). New paradigms for diversifying faculty and staff in higher education: Uncovering cultural biases in the search and hiring process. *Multicultural Education, 14*(2), 65–69.

Mong, S., & Roscigno, V. (2010). African American men and the experience of employment discrimination. *Qualitative Sociology, 33*(1), 1–21.

Palmer, G. A., & Johnson-Bailey, J. (2005). The career development of African Americans in training and organizational development. *Human Resource Planning, 28*(1), 11–12.

Pascarella, E. T., & Terenzini, P. T. (1991). *How college affects students: Findings and insights from twenty years of research.* San Francisco, CA: Jossey-Bass

Phillips, R. (2002). Recruiting and retaining a diverse workforce. *Planning for Higher Education, 30*(4), 32–39.

ACKNOWLEDGMENTS

Editing this book has been a surreal, inspiring, and rewarding experience for us. Doing it with a wonderful friend and colleague only made the experience more special. We can certainly attest to the value of sisterhood and friendship. Maintaining commitment and stamina despite competing demands for our time and life's obstacles was difficult at times, but together, we persevered.

There are individuals to whom we extend a special thanks for their roles throughout the many hours we dedicated to completing this book.

A special thanks to Dr. Donna Ford for her dedication to and advancing research about professionals of color in the academy and for showcasing her expertise. In addition, we appreciate her vision and the wonderful opportunity to create this medium for professionals of color in student affairs to have a voice about their experiences. Dr. Ford's unwavering support and advice were essential and appreciated.

Our sincere gratitude is extended to our children—Nicole Wright, daughter of Dr. Robinson, and Evan and Kyle Burke, the sons of Dr. Burke—for their encouragement, patience, and love through all the many hours we had to give to reading, organizing, and editing.

Thanks to Dr. Robinson's former graduate assistants, Sahar Khan and Melissa Cornejo, for serving as an extra set of eyes.

Thanks to Tim Nichols for his support over the many months Dr. Robinson dedicated to this project.

Much appreciation goes to Dr. Colin Cannonier for being a sounding board and a listening ear for Dr. Burke throughout the process of the project.

Thanks also to LaMarcus Hall for his support of this project.

We are extremely grateful to the contributing authors, who were vulnerable and yet brave, for sharing their truths. Your stories are inspiring, relevant, and highlight a reality that is rarely discussed in the larger realm of scholarship in the field of student affairs.

The journey for professionals of color in higher education can sometimes be arduous as much as it is rewarding. Let us not become weary in doing good, for at the proper time we will reap a harvest if we do not give up (Galatians 6:9, NIV). Onward and upward!

—Monica Galloway Burke
U. Monique Robinson

A CHANGE IS GONNA COME

There have been times that I thought I couldn't last for long
But now I think I'm able to carry on
It's been a long, a long time coming
But I know a change is gonna come, oh yes it will.

—Sam Cooke

In his seminal song, *A Change Is Gonna Come*, Sam Cooke laments about the hardships and fears experienced by Blacks in 1960s America. The song refers to overcoming struggles and adversities while waiting for a change to come as Blacks were working for equality in society, even though they were being continuously subjugated to the daily distresses of racism and discrimination.

This volume includes chapters composed by new and entry-level student affairs professional of color with less than five years in the field. The authors share challenges and changes encountered as they grow professionally, while sometimes working in hostile and culturally assaultive environments, can be accompanied by a multitude of feelings—uncertainty, tension, and triumph. By contextualizing what professionals of color in student affairs experience in their careers, their voices become powerful through sharing with others their struggles, victories, and lessons as exemplified in the following narratives.

CHAPTER 1

FIRST YET ALWAYS LAST

First-Generation Professionals of Color Experiences in Higher Education

Harold E. Brown
Vanderbilt University

Contrary to what many may believe, first-generation status is on a continuum and follows students as they persist and matriculate into their graduate work and, later their professional lives. When these students become new professionals, they attempt to navigate their status within workplace culture while trying to show up as a capable, confident, and competent professional. This process is further complicated when considering the experiences of professionals of color, particularly within the field of higher education. This chapter will examine the many obstacles and professional experiences faced by first-generation professionals of color (FGPOCs). Understanding these experiences and challenges creates an opportunity for institutions to reflect critically on the ways in which they recruit, retain, and support FGPOCs.

Over the past decades, the landscape of higher education has evolved significantly in the way that access is created for students of color. Many universities and colleges have made (or are beginning to make) access an

No Ways Tired, pages 3–10
Copyright © 2019 by Information Age Publishing

institutional priority to manifest a more diverse campus environment that is reflective of a variety of student populations from numerous backgrounds and social classes. Amongst such student populations are those who are the first in their families to pursue postsecondary education—known as first-generation students (FGS). According to Hertel, "approximately 27% of high school graduates in the United States [were] considered first-genera-tion college students" (as cited in Owens, Lacey, Rawls, & Holbert-Quince, 2010, p. 292). While the persistence of first-generation students looks dif-ferent in comparison to their non-first-generation peers, researchers and practitioners identified that persistence for FGS of color is also different when compared to their White non-first-generation counterparts. As a re-sult, many universities and colleges re-examined the ways in which they sup-port first-generation students, while also helping them persist toward the completion of their undergraduate degree. Yet, after first-generation stu-dents of color graduate and, for some, matriculate into graduate programs, their status persists while their narrative is lost.

Moreover, first-generation status for professionals of color can remain a salient part of their identity in their careers and, in some cases, present itself as a barrier to their progression. Within the student affairs workforce, there are new professionals of color who hold first-generation status. For this chapter, I will reference them as first-generation professionals of color (FGPOC). Unfortunately, there is a deficit in literature examining the ex-periences and challenges of FGPOCs within higher education and student affairs. As a FGPOC, it is my hope that this chapter moves the pendulum forward for this population.

CONTINUITY OF FIRST-GENERATION STATUS

At first glance, I was unaware of the continuity of my status. While in col-lege, my first-generation status was not as salient in my day-to-day naviga-tion of campus life. The only time my first-generation status would become more visible than other aspects of my identity would be when I utilized some of the resources in the TRIO Programs Office. Beyond that, my first-generation status did not seem different or isolating because I had other peers who shared the same status. Applying to graduate school was when I, for the first time, saw my status as a deficiency. Contrary to my initial under-standing as a graduating senior, applying to a graduate program worked on a vastly different timeline than that of an undergraduate program. Unfortu-nately, I was not enlightened to this notion until a few months before gradu-ating. For first-generation students of color, particularly those matriculating into graduate programs, there was peer pressure to exhibit a high level of resiliency while operating independently. However, with the help of some professional mentors and a close friend, I persevered and gained admittance into a graduate program for higher education.

Understanding the unique nuances of transition to graduate school in another state was something that took some adjustment. Matriculating onto a new campus with a new culture, quite possibly in a new state, can be initially overwhelming, especially for FGS without any immediate family member(s) who have experience with graduate school. Many FGS of color in graduate programs do not perceive failure as an option. I believed that my graduate school success was inextricably tied to the success of my family. It was a constant battle to understand the jargon and nuances of the curriculum while trying to appear academically and professionally "in the loop" just as much as my classmates. Having student support services such as TRIO on the graduate level would have been ideal in my initial adjustment as an out-of-state FGS of color. Rather, I acclimated to the academic rigor through trial and error and by adopting a different study regimen. However, responsibilities, such as medical insurance, taxes, financial management, and housing, were all things I did not have the appropriate amount of context or knowledge to effectively navigate. This awareness was an immediate reminder of my first-generation status. Once I graduated with a secured job opportunity, and now a second degree in hand, I was ready to take the first step in my professional journey—or so I thought.

THE BURDEN OF IMPOSTER SYNDROME

Immediately after completing my master's degree, I started my role in fraternity and sorority life at a predominantly White institution (PWI). While I was excited to work at an institution held in high regard, the pressure to perform as a "seasoned professional" consistently loomed in the back of my mind. Like many new professionals of color, especially those with first-generation status, it can be a self-imposed expectation to over-perform to compensate for a rationalized "deficit." Consequently, I immediately found myself captured in the grasp of imposter syndrome—when "a person doesn't feel good enough, is unsure of what he's/she's doing, and feels he/she can't live up to others' expectations" (Sherman, 2013, p. 1).

It is important to understand that perception is critical in the orientation and acclimation of FGPOCs in predominantly White work environments. FGPOCs are constantly fighting this fear of "being found out" while trying to affirm to themselves and others of their qualifications to be in that space. This level of awareness can be toxic and quickly evolve into hyper-vigilance. Hyper-vigilance initiated in response to imposter syndrome fosters anxiety that affects professional endurance, resiliency, and mental wellness.

CRACKING THE CODE OF CODE SWITCHING

Code switching, for many professionals of color, serves as a conduit between two realities. One reality is positioned near individual understanding, perception, and norms implicated by cultural experiences; while the other reality is positioned near societal understanding, perception, and norms that intersect with White respectability politics and the desire to appear "cultured and refined" equally to colleagues. Code switching is defined as "the practice of selecting or altering linguistic elements so as to contextualize talk in interaction" (Nilep, 2006, p. 1). For FGPOCs in any industry, code switching can become severely mentally and emotionally taxing. Working in an industry where you are encouraged to bring your most authentic self to the table can be empowering and uplifting. Dually, it can also be anxiety-inducing as it is often unclear if the people you work with find your authentic and palatable. Certainly, I am not asserting that White professionals are incapable of digesting the multifaceted complexities of being a professional of color; however, it is important to acknowledge that institutional and workplace culture can leave an FGPOC feeling more marginalized than before. Oftentimes, acclimation for employees is relegated to a new employee orientation as the sole source of adjustment for new professionals. In addition, there are typically limited support systems for professionals of color, much less for FGPOCs. This is furthered contextualized when considering the campus culture, climate, and constituents. Working at a PWI where many students are from affluent backgrounds with families comprised of generations of alums can emphatically mandate understanding institutional politics and "the way things have been traditionally done." Longwell-Grice, Adsitt, Mullins, and Serrata (2016) conducted qualitative research that examined the experiences of FGS as they navigated their respective campuses. A common theme of "cultural dislocation" emerged after interviewing 14 first-generation students (p. 37).

It can be inferred that cultural dislocation is synonymous with the experiences of FGPOC within the professional culture of higher education. Longwell-Grice et al. (2016) further explained the continuous feeling of marginalization because of the intersection of status and social class. Code switching can serve as a defense mechanism for FGS to cope with adjustment to an institutional environment that is unfamiliar. Olson (2016) conducted a phenomenological study on the transition of first-generation graduates into workplace culture, where one of the participants discussed her experience dealing with the office politics and trying to learn "how to play the system":

> I have learned people's personalities and what makes them happy and how to work within those parameters [...] I hope without sacrificing too much of

myself yet. There are times where I've realized, wow, I would have never, ever done this [...] four years ago. [...] That would have been sacrificing who I was. And today I do it because it's survival. It's how you keep your job and keep your sanity. (p. 363)

This recount demonstrates the necessity of code switching to navigate workplace dynamics and professional sustainability, even if it is at the expense of one's values or ideals. Thus, an authentic self is repetitively conflicting with the professional self in spaces that provide little room for the two to coexist organically.

THE NECESSITY OF FAMILIAL SUPPORT

For many first-generation students, family is a key factor in their persistence and motivation in academia and professional career(s). Family, for this chapter, can refer to biological relatives, legal guardians, and friends. According to Constantine, Wallace, and Kindaichi (as cited in Raque-Bogdan & Lucas, 2016), parental support plays significant part in the career development and outcomes of minorities. Thus, the professional experience can become more challenging when FGPOC families are not equipped financially or emotionally to support new professionals.

It is not unusual for professionals of color to extend their job search to various regions with the impetus of gaining new experiences and appropriate compensation for the knowledge and skills they possess. For many, this milestone of independence personifies the perseverance demonstrated to get this far. Yet, for some, this newly found sense of independence will evolve into homesickness and a yearning to be around their familial support systems.

In 2005 and 2016, I lost my mother and father respectively. While I was a 13-year-old student at the time of my mother's death, I was 24-years old with my master's and 3 weeks into my first professional role when my father died. This unexpected life event caused me to be in my hometown for a month to deal with grief, arrangements, and resolution of the estate. Upon my return to work, I attempted to navigate the impact of my absence on the adjustment to my new position. Due to the change in my family dynamic, I became closer with my remaining family while discovering that the existing void created after my mother's death had then been expanded; thus, leaving me without what I would consider to be my familial support system. The only recourse was to attempt to adjust to my new normal. Unfortunately, in the coming months, I would deal with ongoing grief, insecurities related to my job performance, a self-imposed pressure to figure out the next chapter of my career, and trying to establish an appropriate work–life balance.

Recognizing the influence of family and the impact on performance and adjustment for FGPOCs can lend a broader consideration of other factors. For example, FGPOCs often come from working class families who still struggle to thrive financially. Therefore, many FGPOCs may find that part of their income contributes to the stabilization of their families. This circumstance is important to consider when looking at salaries, professional development allotments, procurement privileges, last-minute expenditures, and the reimbursement process from an institution. Moreover, being the most formally educated person in a family can leave you susceptible to unspoken and assumed financial obligations that may arise amid managing personal and professional responsibilities. Undoubtedly, I found myself taking on a part-time job to offset additional expenses that had arisen after my father's passing. Due to the limitations of funding at many institutions, it would be unreasonable to contend that an unlimited amount of money be allocated for FGPOCs. However, it should be the goal of an institution or department to be aware of the various ways in which FGPOCs' finances can be tied to their family. This acknowledgment emphasizes the need for supervisors and institutions to find creative ways to incorporate familial support into the overall morale and satisfaction of its' FGPOCs within predominantly White spaces.

MOVING FORWARD

I framed my narrative around my choice to self-disclose my first-generation status as a professional of color. First-generations status, for some, may not be the most salient aspect of their identity. Thus, it is important to be cautious with assumptions and stigmas in workplace culture.

Consider the following recommendations as tips that can assist an FGPOC in navigating spaces within higher education. These recommendations are not a "silver bullet" to improving the lived experiences of FGPOCs. Yet, institutions, administrators, and practitioners should evaluate their responsibility in fostering a supportive environment for professionals of color.

Research demonstrates that belonging and community are integral in the adjustment of an individual into a new environment. However, it is uncertain if these factors will be provided or easily identifiable within certain spaces. Thus, FGPOCs should actively seek a consistent and encouraging group of peers who are relatable, reliable, and reaffirming. These relationships can be built on mentorship, friendship, or colleagueship. Furthermore, I recommend that the group should be comprised of individuals inside and outside the career field as to not find oneself constantly surrounded by the woes of the workplace. Collectively, this group helps to create a multidimensional network of support and community that strengthens professional morale and endurance. As an FGPOC, I must underscore that establishing a support system of any capacity is not instantaneous nor is it finite. As FGPOCs evolve and grow, so should their support group(s).

While it is an unreasonable attempt to alleviate the innate reaction to code switch within the workplace, FGPOCs should be confident and unapologetic in their personal values, beliefs, traits, or experiences. Balance is key. For professionals of color, code switching, to an extent, is a necessary defense mechanism within certain environments. However, I recommend that locating certain spaces where code switching is not a necessity can help strike personal balance. I have identified my institution's Black cultural center as a consistent space where I can exist without code switching. If FGPOCs are unable to identify an existing space, they should take the liberty of creating one. Utilizing personal office space to highlight neglected aspects of an individual's identity is a creative way to create an authentic space free of code switching. As a result, you may discover that your personal space serves students in the same way it is intended to serve you.

Lastly, I recommend that FGPOCs be flexible in how they maintain familial support. Depending on proximity, familial support may be a more significant challenge for some than others. In my experience, it has been a true give and take. I have had to truly reflect on what maintaining a level of familial support looks like for me. Understand that familial support may look differently for another FGPOC. Sometimes, it is necessary for me to book a flight or drive 9 or more hours. If I am in town for business, I strategically make plans to see friends and family if my schedule allows. Other times, I try to communicate with and update my friends and family through calls, text, and social media platforms like Facebook and Instagram. I also welcome friends and family to come visit as that may be a feasible option for some. Family and friends should not be sacrificed while in pursuit of a career, if FGPOCs are adaptable and deliberative when ideal.

Collectively, these strategies can be effective in discouraging FGPOCs from viewing their status as a professional deficit, while also empowering and supporting their experiences in relevant ways. If the field of higher education desires more inclusion of other characteristics of identity, we must recognize that first-generation status is on a continuum. By doing so, professionals and institutions have an opportunity to generate dialogue about what support for current and emerging FGPOCs will look like in the coming years.

REFERENCES

Longwell-Grice, R., Adsitt, N. Z., Mullins, K., & Serrata, W. (2016). The first ones: Three studies on first-generation college students. *NACADA Journal, 36*(2), 34–46.

Nilep, C. (2006). Code switching in sociocultural linguistics. *Colorado Research in Linguistics, 19,* 1–22.

Olson, J. S. (2016). Chasing a passion: First-generation college graduates at work. *Emerald Insight, 58*(4), 358–371.

Owens, D., Lacey, K., Rawls, G., & Holbert-Quince, J. (2010). First-generation African American male college students: Implications for career counselors. *The Career Development Quarterly, 58,* 291–300.

Raque-Bogdan, T. L., & Lucas, M. S. (2016). Career aspirations and the first-generation student: Unraveling the layers with social cognitive career theory. *Journal of College Student Development, 57*(3), 248–262.

Sherman, R. O. (2013). Imposter syndrome: When you feel like you're faking it. *American Nurse Today, 8*(5), 57–58.

CHAPTER 2

ON WHOSE BEHALF I THRIVE?
IN WHOSE VOICE I SPEAK?

Hoa Dieu Bui (Bùi Diệu Hoa)
La Salle University

As a student affairs professional of color without American citizenship, the author interrogates the concept of thriving through the multiple narratives and assumptions perpetuated in the American public repertoire about immigrants and international workers. Even though the institution might be supportive to Hoa Bui with all the complexities of her legal status, the general unwelcoming atmosphere of the country toward immigrants and the lack of proactive activism within her own community are challenging. The author calls for the awareness of systemic oppression while encouraging self-advocacy through strategic daily activism. The author proposes polarity thinking as the general mindset to practice individual control and call for more institutional support of one's identity.

Although a Hanoian born and raised, I would make the worst Hanoi tour guide. The Hanoi that I would show will be mundane and even unsightly—a tucked-away market at dawn where vendors slaughter chickens and fishes on demand, a Starbucks with a menu catered to the local taste buds, a street clogged with motorbikes that selectively follow traffic signs and lights, and

No Ways Tired, pages 11–20

a river strangled by renovated houses and trash. My middle-class sheltered upbringing gave me a romanticized, distorted view of my hometown; even the ugliest or most annoying becomes quirkily charming. Groomed carefully for a "better" life elsewhere, when I finally reached the age to face the alleged dehumanization and cutthroats of Hanoi, I left for a fancy liberal arts American education.

If I am awful at showing off Hanoi, I am worse with American universities. For all my 8 years in the United States, from a college student to a resident director, I have exclusively lived on campuses. Like tourists, prospective parents and students visit a university to be awed by the beauty and overwhelmed by the wonder of the pinnacle of academic excellence. As a student affairs professional of color who started as a student activist, I would struggle to give a tour without showing some cynicism about the pervasiveness of Whiteness, the rising cost with higher rates of debt, and the corporatization of higher education. Whiteness presents itself aesthetically, especially as most of the pictures of past leadership on the wall are that of old White men (Plummer, 2003). Interpersonally, students and staff of color can also talk for days about examples of racist and sexist microaggression perpetuated by other students and other staff (Palmer & Maramba, 2015; Solorzano, Ceja, & Yosso, 2000). Structurally, a lack of institutional resources for offices such as the diversity office, international student office, student counseling center, and others prevent adequate support to their students and educational opportunities for the rest of campus. No wonder many predominantly White institutions struggle to retain students of color, especially Black students (Harper, 2006; McClain & Perry, 2017). I am a realist critical of the ivory tower allure.

When other people hear these criticisms, I overwhelmingly receive this response: "Then why are you here? If you don't like it, why don't you just leave?" This is a coded way of saying "Go back where you came from!" These statements carry a set of assumptions and standards for "people like me"—supposedly, for a successful, thriving Asian non-U.S. citizen who is a high-skilled worker and intellectual of color:

- The outcome of somebody staying or leaving the United States is a matter of personal choice.
- To exist in somebody else's country as a person of color naturally means that you must appreciate everything about this country (conversely, if you do not like something about this country, you should leave).

A self-proclamation of thriving leads to a lot of self-doubt and imposter syndrome symptoms. My salary is not six figures. I have a small savings, but it is nowhere near the drop-everything-and-travel-the-world nest egg. As a resident director, I live where I work. Weekly routine "catastrophes" (e.g., unhappy parents, inconsiderate roommate conflict, disagreement among resident assistant staff) and actual catastrophes (e.g., sexual assault, suicidal ideation, mental health crises, intolerant incident, etc.) often surface, which keeps me busy. I do my job quite well—high proficiency and low maintenance—as confirmed by my supervisor. Most of my time is spent in one-on-one meetings, staff meetings, team meetings, committee meetings, or department meetings. None of these aspects of my life is particularly riveting, yet they sustain my basic needs. Additionally, I take pride in the mentality that I have developed to take responsibility for my life, while speaking out against this country's political hostility toward foreigners. Thriving is both a condition of life and a mindset.

GO BACK WHERE YOU CAME FROM

A scorching late summer day of my sophomore year, I was at a campus bus stop with my roommate on route to the grocery store. Along with a flowy summer dress and a beach hat, I also wore my hair in pigtail braids. This whimsical fashion sense definitely contributed to my feeling out of place at a rural upstate New York liberal arts college. Being Asian with an accent does not help either. On the bus, other than my roommate and me, who is a scrawny Asian American girl, is the bus driver who is a White male in his late 40s. As I throw my sweaty self on the leather bench, I let out a loud "Ugh! Why is it so hot?" The driver exchanged a customary nod with us. He then turns toward me with amusement on his face and asks, "Oh yeah! You think this is hot?" I meekly affirm, "Oh, for sure. I am sweating like crazy!" "Ha, then where are you from?" he inquires. "Hmmm . . . Vietnam," I answer and look to the window, hoping he would lose interest. Then, he went where I anticipated. With a smirk, he replied, "So you think this is hot? Why don't you go back to your rice field? Isn't it hot there, too?" I pretended not to hear him, turned to my roommate, whose consciousness was totally consumed by an iPhone game, and our shopping list. Not acknowledging that interaction (microaggression) minimizes the pain.

I will start calling this group of people "U.S. expats," short for expatriates, to reverse a racist colonial narrative that calls every person of color living in another country different from their country of origin, regardless of success level or income, "immigrant" or "migrant." Often "expat" is reserved exclusively for White elite people (Koutoni, 2015; Nash, 2017). "Go back" plagues the life and vocabulary of international students and employees in the United States. Whenever I ask my expat students and friends where they are going for breaks, they would automatically say, "Oh, I am going *back.*" Then, I give them a confused look, so they clarify, "To China/ Vietnam/Angola, and so forth." Instead of "going back," they could have said "going home." Just as every college senior dreads the question "What are you going to do after you graduate?" every U.S. expat dreads, "Are you going *back* to [X country]?" or "Are you going to stay in the United States?" While this kind of questioning is generally legitimate and fair, it *might* be contextually offensive and a microaggression. The agony evoked by the question does not make its offensiveness inherent. If anything, the question carries an (excusable) insouciance of the complexity of the U.S. immigration system, an assumption of an expat's ability to choose to stay or leave and a privileged sense of entitlement of and to the land.

I am on the H-1B visa, reserved for highly-skilled foreign workers, which is very competitive, as the number of applicants is always a few times more than that of available visas. In 2017, 1 month before the opening date on the visa petition, the United States Citizenship and Immigration Services (USCIS) announced that, starting April 3, it will "temporarily suspend premium processing for all H-1B petitions" and this might last for 6 months (USCIS, 2017). This premium processing is an additional service with a $1,225 fee and applicants will know if their petition is approved within 2 weeks as opposed to 6 months. This halt created a backlog for all applicants, so it could be much longer to get the results and many—myself included—might fall out of legal status. I had 1 month to put in paperwork to apply for the premium processing or risk not having work authorization altogether. A few days after the notice came out in the news, I learned of the announcement (not from the university's general counsel), and spiraled into despair. I began to think I was becoming more and more expensive for the institution. Some institutions do not even read résumés from some applicants due to this visa situation (the online application always asks). For a long time, I lived on "conditional hospitality," which is when "you are welcomed on condition that you give something back in return" (Ahmed, 2012, p. 43). The original petition fee came from my department budget and, now, an unexpected additional $1225 is required. Just as the participants in Dhaliwal and Forkert's (2015) study, I played the deserving immigrant game and employed respectability politics by playing into the model immigrant stereotype of hyper-productivity (which jeopardized the delicate work-life balance of a live-in professional). Supposedly, the goals are to weed out the undeserving immigrants (in the "innocent post-racial" description this means not speaking English, lazy, uneducated, low skill, criminal, mooching off the system, etc.). The game rules are demanding and the game is unsatisfying for losers.

The morning after learning about the additional cost, when asking my department whether they are willing to pay for the additional fee, I apologized to my supervisor for being a burden. Not missing a beat, my supervisor said, "As an institution, we support who you are and this is what we have to do." I felt supported, yet still guilty. I expressed this guilt and she told me,

"You are an investment." All my life as a U.S. expat, I always felt like I was living on borrowed time, stolen land, and lent money (i.e., on financial aid thorough college and graduate school and in need of visa sponsorship for work). Not once did I consider that I could be an investment, an integral part of an organization, rather than a guest who must prove worthiness upfront. I was fortunate enough that my department was willing to pay the extra fee and go the extra distance to file my petition before the deadline. However, outside of my department, the discourse that "illegal" immigrants are leeching off the system and foreign workers are taking American jobs, is going strong. Let's not forget the multiple reiterations (albeit fail) of the travel ban since January and the announcement of the end of the Deferred Action for Childhood Arrivals (DACA) program in September 2017. Just recently, the Department of Homeland Security ended the Temporary Protection Program benefiting 200,000 Salvadorans living in the United States for 17 years and their U.S.-born children (Jordan, 2018). Regardless of the relationship between our home country with the United States at the time, U.S. expats know that the rug under our feet can be pulled at any point and us expats will have to "go back." This understanding is especially true for U.S. expats of color (see Raff, 2017).

WITH GREAT(?!) POWER COMES GREAT (ERASURE) OF RESPONSIBILITY

What do I owe this land and the people that contribute to the most formative years of my early adult life? What grants me the entitlement that I can and should speak back to its oppressive environment? With what authority do I show up at Black Lives Matter protests and speak out against anti-Blackness and White supremacy? When I show up to a rally, an anti-racism conference, or a social justice workshop (that is not Asian-specific), I am generally one of the few Asian-looking people present. Sometimes, I wonder if the model minority, along with a few collateral benefits, wraps the psyche of Asian Americans and Asian immigrants so tightly that only a few of us extend our political solidarity to other Black and Brown folks and wield our political power. Beside the psychological pressure it places on many Asian and Asian American children to always conform, be quiet, and be academically high-achieving, the model minority myth causes a serious case of historical amnesia. Asian and Asian American students do not learn the death of Vincent Chin, the heroic Yuri Kochiyama and Grace Lee Boggs, the vast body of radical literature and arts made by Trinh Thi Minh Ha, or the sustained relationship between Asians 4 Black Lives group with Black Lives Matter organizers. Additionally, examples of racism against Asian and Asian Americans within student affairs often stop at microaggressions and the perception of the perpetual foreigners, which are indeed harmful but incomplete and unhelpful. It is hard to join a conversation on police brutality and school-to-prison pipeline when statistics of these issues on Asian American do not exist. When a history and a reality are erased from a people's consciousness and society constantly pushes them toward the direction of the model minority, no wonder Asian Americans internalize and justify their invisibility. Without political integrity and a firm extensive grasp of the (thin) literature, one can easily fall into the Oppression Olympics mindset, comparing the oppression of one group to another. This reaction becomes a feedback loop—the lack of Asian/Asian American presence in political conversation in student affairs further effaces the history and strengthens the model minority myth inside and outside of the Asian/Asian American community.

A year ago, I attended a founding meeting of the organization for Asian/Asian American faculty and staff at my predominantly White institution. When going around the room to ask what the 20 people there expect from the group, we received 20 different answers from "just meeting new people" to "learn more about the resources at the school" to "fight against daily oppression of our people." The person calling the meeting was at a loss for words and admitted that she did not know where to go from there; no theme emerged for her to start. A sad silence drenched the air momentarily. Later in the same meeting, a female faculty member in her early 30s brought up the issue of the tenure track not recognizing community and student-care work, which female professors of color have to do a lot due to their identity. Immediately, a male professor in his 60s jumped in and mansplained to her the tenure criteria, as if she were a graduate student, telling her to do more research and be a good teacher. In that brief moment when I considered jumping in to call out the ridiculous sexist microaggression, I considered the social expectation embedded in my young Asian femaleness (compared to that of an older Asian man) *and* the professional expectation written in my entry-level student affairs staff position (compared to that of a tenured professor). I decided to bite my tongue.

My identity as a visible woman of color, my *being*, is intricately linked with my work, my *doing*. Ahmed (2012) made a distinction between "those employed as diversity workers *(doing diversity)* or those who arrival is coded as sign of diversity, such as people of color *(being diversity)*" (p. 49). Ahmed argued "those of us of color [diversity practitioners] are already diversity before we do diversity, such that our doing is often read as being" (p. 196). Reversely, my *being* is my *doing*. This reality creeps in my student affairs work. Here is an example. Roommate conflicts happen, even among those of seemingly shared backgrounds. However, an aversion toward a domestic-international roommate pair exists. I have heard, multiple times, American parents and domestic and international students requesting a different room assignment *before* the school year starts. I once had to take care of a roommate conflict between an American student and a Korean student. The situation was typical— different schedules, noise, room temperature, lack of communication, and so on. The parents of the domestic student were already involved, demanding a swift course of action to take their son out of his misery (parents of international students typically never contact us). In a phone call, I told the parents what I would have told any parent in that situation, "To resolve the situation, I would need to talk to the students and coach them through the roommate agreement and the mediation process." Months later, long after the situation's resolution, I learned from my supervisor that the parent demanded somebody else handle this conflict because she was afraid that, as a foreigner (she heard my foreigner-ness on the phone), I would be biased against her son and side with the Korean student. Because of my "being" a diverse individual and possessing the little bit of authority given by the institution, many assume that I have much power to actively promote "diversity" or "reverse racism." Since then, I have had more domestic students and parents insinuating or flat out saying similar comments. Deeply buried pain spills over still whenever I think of this situation because a proxy of Whiteness and "true" Americanness is what allowed me to do my job. On the other hand, I also had international students ask me to let them get away with policy violations because, "We (me and them) are from the same culture" (we definitely are not) or "It [documenting the violation] is going to look bad for us, the Asians."

TOWARD A LIVABLE STRATEGY
FOR A LIFETIME OF UNSOLVABLES

bell hooks (2014) wrote, "To critique sexist images without offering alternatives is an incomplete intervention. Critique in and of itself does not lead to change" (p. 35). Rather than being helpful, my above narrative might lead to more cynicism, helplessness, and confusion for both U.S. expats and non-expat higher education administrators. The alternative I suggest is an approach called "polarity thinking" to maintain sanity, while doing the day-to-day work and keeping an eye on the bigger social contexts (e.g., immigration discourses and regulations, racism, sexism, etc.). These bigger "isms" are "unsolvable" because I do not see these issues being resolved within my lifetime. However, my life is still worth living and I must use polarity thinking to get on with my life. Polarity thinking serves as the central framework for my recommendations.

Johnson (1992) coined polarity thinking, which is an approach that seeks to manage the dynamic relationship between two polarities to maximize the positives and minimize the negatives of both. A few popular examples of polarities in higher education is *challenge* versus *support; people-first approach* versus *administration-first approach; being a flexible supervisor* versus *being a clear cut one; individual-focus work* versus *team-focus work;* and *individual autonomy* versus *departmental consistency.* These examples are polarities because they exist interdependently with one another, both have positives and negatives, and are equally valid and important for the life of an individual or an organization. An intuitive polarity example is inhaling and exhaling—opposite processes, yet both are conditional for each other's function and critical for biological survival. The smooth alternating transition between inhaling and exhaling creates an infinite close loop that facilitates growth. Johnson (1992) also contended that conceptualizing all issues as "problems to solve" is detrimental to individuals or organizations because there are unsolvable problems. One way to identify an unsolvable problem is when, after a long discussion, people shrug and comment, "Well, we just need to find a balance." In the language of polarity thinking, finding this elusive "balance" is to recognize that some life problems are caused by the push and pull of these polarities and managing them rather than solving them. One does not "solve" breathing problems with only inhaling or exhaling. Managing breathing is to inhale deeply and exhale fully in a controlled rhythm.

One polarity pair relevant to the life of U.S. expats of color in higher education is *asserting individual control* versus *demanding institutional support.* I have an individual control for knowing the details and requirements of my immigration status and the H-1B visa, challenging other Asian expats to be more socially conscious, and conducting myself in the best of my ability so that parents do not suspect any professional incompetency. However, since my struggles are due to my social identities and social systems I do not have control over, other components—the institution, my department, my direct and indirect supervisors, and the university at large—also have a responsibility to provide structured support and resources so that I can devote my time and energy to the institution rather than worry about my legal status, my activism, or hostile attitudes. To only assert individual control and not expect institutional support is setting oneself up for failure, loneliness, and burn out. To expect institutional support without taking ownership of one's life is irresponsible to oneself and unhelpful for the institution because an institution cannot possibly know everything its employees need. Managing one's expectations for oneself and the institution is necessary to gain control of one's life without absolving the institution or system of its responsibility.

RECOMMENDATIONS

While success has its external (i.e., objective) side, such as income or academic achievement, thriving is also an internal concept and a state of mind—to be able to sleep at night, to not feel oneself as a walking contradiction, and to not see an imposter in the mirror every morning. Managing this polarity pair well does not mean that one day I will miraculously become a proud campus tour guide; however, it keeps me focused and away from both painful self-blame and destructive futility.

I have established a support network to navigate the complex and political process of seeking employment as an expat of color. I have reached out to other expats at schools that I applied to about institutional support and not shying away from bringing expat-related issues to my supervisor early and directly. As I remain updated with new legislations and laws, I expect institutions to support me by communicating when a mismatch exists between what an institution says it will do and what actually happens. For example, when I transitioned between the student visa and the working visa and needed legal support, my in-between position caused a lot of ball-passing to occur between the human resources office and the international student services office. Pointing this out did not get me the support I needed because the institution had reached its limit, yet the institution learned that there is a gap in its support for other future expat employees and students.

This mentality also informs my activist work, even when activism does not fit the deversing immigrant discourse and it might invoke more of the "go back to where you came from" sentiment and statements from others. I have started to write and publish my writings on the experiences of student affairs expat professionals and this is a way to counteract the insidious influence of the model minority myth. Writing this story is my way of continuing the legacy and contributing to the possibility of strong Asian/Asian American voices in student affairs and the political climate at large. As I reflect on my own frustration related to my identity, I have learned to accept and embrace that my success is intricately connected to how others in my community succeed. Loving my identity as a professional of color means that I cannot think of myself as the odd Asian expat but, rather, as a member of a beloved diverse larger community with flaws and strengths and so much potential.

REFERENCES

Ahmed, S. (2012). *On being included: Racism and diversity in institutional life*. Durham, NC: Duke University Press.

Dhaliwal, S., & Forkert, K. (2015). Deserving and undeserving migrants. *Soundings, 61*, 49–61.

Harper, S. (2006). *Black male students at public flagship universities in the U.S.: Status, trends and implications for policy and practice*. Washington, DC: Joint Center for Political and Economic Studies.

hooks, b. (2014). *Feminism is for everybody*. Cambridge, MA: South Press End.

Johnson, B. (1992). *Polarity management: Identifying and managing unsolvable problems.* Amherst, MA: HRD Press.

Jordan, M. (2018, Jan 8). Trump administration says that nearly 200,000 Salvadorans must leave. *The New York Times.* Retrieved from https://www.nytimes.com/2018/01/08/us/salvadorans-tps-end.html?hp&action=click&pgtype=Homepage&clickSource=story-heading&module=first-column-region&region=top-news&WT.nav=top-news&_r=0

Koutoni, M. R. (2015, March 13). Why are White people expats when the rest of us are immigrants? *The Guardian.* Retrieved from https://www.theguardian.com/global-development-professionals-network/2015/mar/13/white-people-expats-immigrants-migration

McClain, K., & Perry, A. (2017). Where did they go: Retention rates for students of color at predominantly White institutions. *College Student Affairs Leadership, 4*(1), 3.

Nash, K. (2017, January 20). *The difference between an expat and an immigrant?* Semantic. *BBC.* Retrieved from http://www.bbc.com/capital/story/20170119-who-should-be-called-an-expat

Palmer, R. T., & Maramba, D. C. (2015). Racial microaggressions among Asian American and Latino/a students at a historically Black university. *Journal of College Student Development, 56*(7), 705–722.

Plummer, D. L. (2003). Diagnosing diversity in organization. In *Handbook of diversity management: Beyond Awareness to Competency Based Learning* (pp. 243–269). Lanham, MD: University Press of America.

Raff, J. (2017). The "double punishment" for Black undocumented immigrants. *The Atlantic.* Retrieved from https://www.theatlantic.com/politics/archive/2017/12/the-double-punishment-for-black-immigrants/549425/

Solorzano, D., Ceja, M., & Yosso, T. (2000). Critical race theory, racial microaggressions, and campus racial climate: The experiences of African American college students. *The Journal of Negro Education, 69,* 60–73.

U.S. Citizenship and Immigration Services. (2017, March 3). USCIS will temporarily suspend premium processing for all H-1B petitions. *U.S. Citizenship and Immigration Services.* Retrieved from https://www.uscis.gov/archive/uscis-will-temporarily-suspend-premium-processing-all-h-1b-petitions

CHAPTER 3

TESTIMONIOS OF ENTRY-LEVEL LATINA/O/X STUDENT AFFAIRS PROFESSIONALS

Karla Cruze-Silva
University of Arizona

Roberto Cruze
University of Arizona

Gary Santos Mendoza
Florida Atlantic University

Through the art of storytelling or testimonios, three entry-level Latina/o/x student affairs professionals share their experiences, challenges, and revelations. Drawing from expectations, motivation, and disapproval from family, colleagues, society and more, these authors explore what it means to them to be a student affairs professional of color and how they have come to persevere through unique challenges.

As entry-level professionals, we constantly navigate new territory often not knowing if the choices we make will be for our betterment or detriment.

No Ways Tired, pages 21–30
Copyright © 2019 by Information Age Publishing

We move through higher education only armed with a limited understanding of what it means to be in higher education. We look to those who came before us for guidance, a sense of comfort, and validation, only to find that there are few people who look like us in higher education, and even fewer in the field of student affairs. Because we have no definitive path or North Star to guide us, we shuffle our way through our careers, trying to find our truths and hoping our shuffling will be enough to guide us towards success.

Literature regarding Latina/o/x professionals in student affairs is slim. Researchers have shown Latina/o/x professionals often experience incidents of microaggression and imposter syndrome (Nadal, Mazzula, Rivera, & Fujii-Doe, 2014). The microaggressions faced by Latina/o/x student affairs professionals can vary greatly, but can be widely defined as, "various types of [intentional or unintentional] daily insults, invalidations, and assaults experienced by Latina/o/[x] Americans" (Nadal et al., 2014, p. 68). What the literature often fails to show is how experiences and their resulting effects on Latina/o/x professionals alter the work and perception of what it means to be a professional Latina/o/x through everyday work. Although literature often fails to show the effect of how we experience working in higher education, a common experience for Latino/a/x professionals in the field often surrounds the need for spaces where Latino/a/x higher education professionals can learn from each other (Matos, 2018). These counterspaces help us understand each other and ourselves, personally and professionally from a cultural lens, and not feel like we are the only ones on our college campuses (West, 2017).

Within most Latina/o/x cultures, storytelling is a highly valuable skill and oftentimes, how wisdom is passed. In this chapter, our storytelling takes the form of our *testimonios*—a tool to share our truths within a system, which systematically oppressed people of color. Each author has unique experiences directly influencing the ways we view the world and how we navigate our professional careers. Although we are three Latina/o/x individuals, it is important to recognize that our identities are unique and how we experience these identities are unique as well. It is unwise and illogical to assume all Latina/o/x individuals share the same experiences as us and we welcome readers to share in our emotional journeys as we attempt to shed light on the complexities of how our identities may intersect.

ROBERTO'S *TESTIMONIO*: COMBATING RACIALIZED PROFESSIONAL EXPECTATIONS

A smart man once told me not to forget where I come from. Although to some people this might seem cliché, for a long time this reminder served as more of a burden, or as Alex Gonzalez shared in his chapter in *Identity and Leadership: Informing Our Lives, Informing Our Leadership,* "a sack of onions on my back" (Chávez & Sanlo, 2013, p. 201). When I first read Alex's *testimonio,* "Shifting Between Worlds Carrying Home on My Back," the first thing I thought was, "Wow, I'm not the only one," yet I still felt alone and not completely understood.

As a professional within higher education, I balance a wide range of expectations from teachers, supervisors, and family to be successful and to know the exact response to every situation, all while being unable to make mistakes because I was one of the good Latinos who "made it." The most burdensome expectation is being accountable for the emotional and psychological discomfort of White colleagues due to aspects of myself I have no control over. Colleagues seemed unable to allow moments of grace during learning moments because, as an educated Latino male, I should have already known better and done better. I remember several situations in my career where I have sat with an "onion sack on my back" (Chávez & Sanlo, 2013, p. 201) trying to balance expectations set upon me by White peers, supervisors, and university leadership while also trying to honor who I am as an individual, not knowing if I was being true to where I come from and who I am. I remember moments when I have felt weighed down by racially charged expectations on how I should or should not have engaged, spoken, looked, stood, sat, or dressed in a specific situation with a student or another professional. Often, it would come in the form of "well-intended constructive feedback" from mostly White female peers that I *took up too much space* or my *tone of voice was too aggressive/confrontational;* even when a White peer would do or say the same and not be given a second glance or even applauded for their assertiveness. When I am passionate or show any excitement about a topic, I am labeled hyper-masculine and aggressive while my White male counterparts who share the same passion and excitement in the same tones receive the designation of passionate advocates.

In my career as a student affairs professional, the most persistent and arduous battle has been combating the racialization of my professionalism. I would be lying if I said it has not influenced how I perform or present myself as a student affairs professional. How colleagues racialized my professionalism can be as covert as mentioning I am intimidating or saying I look "like a thug" when I walked around a residence hall in jeans and university sweater. Such allegations forced me to hide my authentic self and present my whitewashed professional self; all for the sake of saving myself from emotional battles I know I will not win. I have learned as I network professionally, relate to colleagues, try to relate to students, move through campus, or even simply sit in a meeting, I must negotiate how much of my authenticity I can bring to the table. Not for their appeasement or comfort, but to save myself from a battle I did not start and my lack of mental and emotional endurance to fight during every interaction of the day. I verbally and nonverbally adjust myself to seem less intimidating to advocate for and assist students who already have a tough time navigating higher education.

As I have grown and become more confident in my professional ability, I question if what I was taught about being a competent and woke professional is valid. Am I being true to who I am as an individual? Am I being true to where I came from? Is it my responsibility to change when someone is unable to respect characteristics of myself I am not able to control? To what length am I going to internalize the oppressive restraints of what it means to be professional? These are all difficult questions. A mentor and friend taught me to look at a situation and try to understand from where an action, comment, or piece of feedback may be coming. Is it out of genuine care for my performance, fear, misunderstanding, or implicit biases? From there, you must determine for yourself if and how any possible change can result as no one else can give you a definitive answer. To determine your answer, you must be introspective, seek out other's experiences, and challenge your own paradigms to see possibilities you may not have previously considered.

Ultimately, my truth is what makes me a great professional and how I can relate to the students I serve. I should not have to change who I am to be able to interject myself into white spaces. My ability to stay true to myself while helping underrepresented students is my biggest skill—a skill learned from my struggles of others racializing my professionalism and a constant barrage of microaggressions. I am a passionate 1.5 generation White passing Latino male who is true to both who I am and from where I come. My place at the table will help students succeed regardless of how anyone perceives me.

KARLA'S *TESTIMONIO*

I am a Latina, first-generation college graduate, feminist, scholar, activist, and practitioner who is always learning. As Espino, Vega, Rendón, Ranero, and Muñiz (2012) put it, "One form of resistance to these multiple marginalities involves drawing upon and (re)telling one's lived experience to expose oppression and systematic violence" (p. 444). This is my *testimonio* as an entry-level professional.

Ponte las pilas is a phrase my parents told me while I was growing up. It's a phrase they continue to tell me and is constantly in the back of my mind as I navigate my journey in student affairs. To understand my journey, you must understand my past. My parents immigrated from Mexico to *el otro lado* in the 1980s. Each left their *familias* and everything they knew behind. My parents never had the chance to go to college but they worked hard to make going to college a reality for me. I never believed I was good enough to be accepted into a 4-year university and as a first-generation college student, my parents did not know how to help me navigate the college system.

Without much thought during orientation, I signed up to be a part of a first-generation program on campus. This program helped me find a community and provided me with resources and support towards not only graduation, but also finding my passion. By my third year in college, I knew I wanted to go into student affairs.

I next found myself trying to navigate the waters of graduate school but this time, I knew more about the higher education system. I also had my parents saying, *ponte las pilas*. However, all the support and information did not take away the feeling of not being worthy. As I shared the news of my acceptance into an Ivy League graduate program, people would say, "Oh you just got in because you're brown." This remark was usually made in the form of a joke, yet people failed to realize their words had a lasting impact. As someone who already lacked confidence, these comments hurt; I began to doubt myself and even wonder if I was only chosen to meet the program's diversity quota.

We focus so much on students that we often forget professionals from marginalized backgrounds also face many challenges related to finding their spaces on campus. As a professional, it does not become easier to find spaces. In my experience, it becomes more difficult because many times there are political and bureaucratic factors at play. I have had to work twice as hard to find the spaces and communities in which I feel comfortable. Part of being able to feel comfortable in a community is having someone to whom I can relate. Although there is minimal literature that speaks to the need for counter spaces for professionals of color, there is even less literature on the importance of mentoring for women of color in student affairs (Murrell & Blake-Beard, 2017). As a professional, the need for mentors with whom I can identify has become increasingly important. Having a mentor to whom I can talk about work and other important parts of my life, such as being a doctoral student and balancing home and work life, have also proven to make a huge difference. These relationships have helped guide me as well as process the many microaggressions I have experienced and witnessed.

One of the biggest lessons I have learned is that my experiences matter. Who I consider knowledge holders has greatly shifted in the last few years. This shift happened because of the literature and research I have been doing, which shows us how we are all knowledge holders. We usually think of professors or supervisors as knowledge holders but many times we fail to realize our students and entry-level professionals are also knowledge holders. This perspective corresponds with Yosso's (2005) challenge for professionals to think critically about whose knowledge counts and whose is discounted. Yosso (2005) also suggested people of color draw on the capital they bring with them from their homes and communities. Applying theory to our communities can take many shapes and forms and there is no "right" way to practice theory. Many times, professionals of color need to look outside of higher education for theories and/or practices they can use that more accurately reflect our reality. Gloria Anzaldúa (2012), a Chicana feminist scholar, also challenges traditional ways of knowing and calls for our awareness of alternative sources of knowledge to disrupt traditional binaries. These are some examples of researchers who incorporate their own spirituality into their work. This literature gives those who study these works the confidence to use their own experiences in a professional setting.

In many ways, I am still very much like my undergraduate self, constantly finding new ways to navigate this higher education system or to help others navigate it, whether it is by telling my story or being an advocate for students and colleagues. My journey has been plagued by my own self-doubt, microaggressions, and a system that was not created for someone like me. Being a woman of color has impacted the way in which I navigate and view my profession. As I continue this journey of resistance and fight against an oppressive system, I will always remember those three little words—*ponte las pilas*.

GARY'S *TESTIMONIO*

The piece of advice I give my students is to remember where you came from; it shaped you to be who you are. Growing up Latinx, the verse "I've come too far from where I started from. Nobody told me that the road would be easy" (Burrell, 1996, verse 1) is something I identified with and it describes my lived experiences. My community holds strong beliefs about those who identify as Latinx, including expectations of education, work, marriage, and procreation; however, it never allowed for a gay and Latino identity. Morales' (1989) work on gay Latino male identity notes the conflict that occurs through a balancing act to fulfill cultural norms and societal expectations within gay and Latino identity. For me, the imbalance associated with my Latinx identity meant leaving West 108th Street with acknowledgement of my queer identity to move toward my career as a scholar-practitioner. Furthermore, Excelencia in Education (2015) found that .5% of Latinx individuals completed a terminal degree, which added more meaning in my life toward validating my Latinx identity. However, the balancing act of salient but marginalized identities at different points of life could not have been accomplished if it was not for my *Reto* by Choice mentality with the help of my chosen *familia*.

For me, my Puerto Rican/Ecuadorian parents who are from a rough working-class Morningside Heights neighborhood in Manhattan, New York, were my guides. From the weekly *coro* on the stoop outside my parents' tenement apartment to the sounds of salsa and the Yankees from the neighborhood at all hours of the day, this was the space where I spent my formative years developing my Latinx identity. The exploration of my sexual orientation, however, was away from home. Occurring in my early teens, my first queer club experience became an influential moment to me; it led to acceptance of my gay identity. This space of vices and different people, especially meeting others with my similar Latinx identity, gave me the liberation to be comfortable as part of the inner city queer community. The period I call "*La Fiesta*" occurred at a time I felt the lowest in life in regards to my sexual identity. The resources on how to understand my identity were scarce and, until college, I was lost.

While "*La Fiesta*" took over my life during the weekends, during the weekdays I was a student at St. John's University. On those weekends, I met many queer people of color who could not afford or consider college as an option for advancement. Living in New York City meant you knew The Stonewall Inn, the epicenter of progression for queer rights. Even that inspiration was not enough for some in my queer community to not throw their lives away. The desire to change the narrative in my queer community motivated me to be better.

A team building class from the Chaplin School of Hospitality & Tourism Management at Florida International University (FIU) is where I learned the concept of *Reto* by Choice (Challenge by Choice). The model consists of three circles—the first level is your comfort zone; the second is your growth zone; and the outer circle is the danger zone. The goal is to give the individual the option to "Challenge by Choice" by stepping out of their comfort zone into the growth zone to continue growing as an individual. If you reach toward the danger zone, your growth will remain stagnant. The concept of *Reto* by Choice personified my undergraduate experience and motivation in college to get out of my comfort zone and into my own growth zone. Racial/ethnic minority students value the importance of mattering; it provides them a feeling of belonging and capacity to do well at an institution of higher education (Hawkins & Larabee, 2009). *Reto* by Choice ignited leadership opportunities on campus via becoming President of the Latino American Student Organization and at one point of Phi Iota Alpha Fraternity, Inc. Research has shown that participation in student involvement or passion projects contributes to a queer student and their sexual identity development process (Renn & Bilodeau, 2005). Being a figurehead in two Latinx identity organizations provided opportunity for the development of my gay identity and a reconnection with my Latinx identity. This motivation came in part through the forming of my chosen family in college. Five individuals, who I met through my Latinx organization and my fraternity, provided me with motivation, love, and insistent value toward myself. In turn, I helped them overcome shortcomings of identity, insecurity, and confidence. This chosen *familia* aligned my passions with my professional purpose in higher education, including support when I came out as gay or *maricon* to my immediate family. However, the "lifestyle" my Latinx culture dictated became fuel to prove to others that success is limitless, especially if this *maricon* is winning.

Confidence in my identity and support from my families reinforced my decision to move to Florida. In order to celebrate the changes I had undergone and conquer challenges by working in higher education. Ironically, my time in *"La Fiesta"* helped me meet a friend who introduced me to my career in higher education. His conversations about undergraduate involvement indirectly piqued my interest, which inspired me to obtain my master's degree from FIU and to currently pursue a doctorate. *Reto* by Choice, my *familias*, and confidence made me strive to push forward. For me, my experience as a first-generation, queer person of color through my educational journey and professional career is the trail towards giving back to the queer community that accepted me through education, decolonization, and support.

PA'DELANTE

Through each of our journeys, we have struggled, learned, and grown to understand ourselves and the world around us better. Each of our journeys helps inform how we see ourselves as professionals in student affairs, but also helps to illustrate commonalities in how the current cultural norms in the United States of America and our individual communities have placed roadblocks for us to overcome. What is certain is that we cannot become complacent in our understanding of ourselves and how we can become better professionals. Whether you need time for introspection, someone to ask you tough questions, someone to tell you *ponte las pilas*, or the space to receive validation from your *familia*, you must be the author of your own truth. What we have been able to find in our searches for truth are the following:

> *Know and be yourself.* You must stay true to yourself and determine what it means for you to bring your authentic self into your everyday work. Being your authentic self can be the best tool you have when relating to students, particularly through shared identity.
> *Have perseverance.* Higher education is not designed for the success of Latinas/os/x individuals. When something is tough, *ponte las pilas.* Continue to persevere the best way you know how. Remember, you are not the only one, you are not alone, and you are enough.
> *Secure mentorship.* We all need someone to look up to, bounce ideas off, or help us process through work and life experiences. Find that chosen *familia* with whom you can be your true authentic self with and is willing to help you evaluate your blind spots. Stand on the

shoulders of giants while you strive to become one of those giants in student affairs.

Find counter spaces/community. We have all had to negotiate how we show our authentic selves in higher education. Seek out the spaces you need to recharge, re-center, and share in a community that understands you and accepts you for who you are.

Learning on the job. Learn all you can from where you can, but know you are new to the field of student affairs. Understanding that being alert with your job "firsts" is important. The level of work and opportunities you take advantage of will guide future opportunities.

Do not judge a book by its cover. College students are coming in with a wide array of social identities that can be different from yours. Be open to understand before assuming a person's identities. Take the time to get to know their pronoun, language, and racial/ethnic background.

APPENDIX: SPANISH TRANSLATIONS

Coro—A colloquial Spanish word with roots from the Dominican Republic, meaning a group of friends/family coming together to have a fun time, it is used in urban Latinx neighborhoods in the United States of America.

El otro lado—A colloquial Spanish phrase meaning "the other side" mainly used in Mexico in referring to the United States of America.

En union, hay la fuerza—In unity, lies is strength

Familia/Familias—Family

La Fiesta—The Party

Maricon—A derogatory term referring an individual who does not identify as heterosexual.

Pa'delante—Spanish contraction of the words "*Para*" and "*Adelante*" which translates to "moving forward."

Ponte las pilas—A colloquial Spanish phrase roughly translating to "get it together and get to work."

Raices—Roots

Reto—Challenge

Testimonios—The story telling of one's experiences.

REFERENCES

Andalzua, G. (1987). *Borderlands/La frontera: The new mestiza.* San Francisco, CA: Spinster/Aunt Lutte.

Burrell, C. (Composer). (1996). *I don't feel no ways tired* [Sheet Music]. United States of America: Peermusic.

Chavez, A. F., & Sanlo, R. (2013). *Identity and leadership: Informing our lives, informing our practice.* Washington, DC: National Association for Student Personnel Administrators.

Espino, M. M., Vega, I. I., Rendón, L. I., Ranero, J. J., & Muñiz, M. M. (2012). The process of reflexión in bridging testimonios across lived experience. *Equity & Excellence in Education, 45*(3), 444–459.

Excelencia in Education. (2015). *The condition of Latinos in education: 2015 Factbook.* Washington, DC: Author.

Hawkins, V. M., & Larabee, H.J. (2009). Engaging racial/ethnic minority students in cut-of-class activities in predominantly white campuses. In S. Harper (Ed.), *Student engagement in higher education* (pp. 179–197). New York, NY: Routledge.

Matos, J. C. (2018). Using "I" statements. In A. E. Batista (Ed.), *Latinx/a/os in higher education: Exploring identity, pathways, and success* (pp. 179–187). Washington, DC: National Association of Student Personnel Administrators, Inc.

Morales, E. S. (1989). Ethnic minority families and minority gays and lesbians. *Marriage & Family Review, 14*(3–4), 217–239.

Murrell, A. J., & Blake-Beard, S. (2017). *Mentoring diverse leaders: Creating change for people, processes, and paradigms.* New York, NY: Routledge.

Nadal, K. L., Mazzula, S. L., Rivera, D. P., & Fujii-Doe, W. (2014). Microaggressions and Latina/o Americans: An analysis of nativity, gender, and ethnicity. *Journal of Latina/o Psychology, 2*(2), 67–78.

Renn, K. A., & Bilodeau, B. (2005). Queer student leaders: An exploratory case study of identity development and LGBT student involvement at a Midwestern research university. *Journal of Gay & Lesbian Issues in Education, 2*(4), 49–71. https://doi.org/10.1300/J367v02n04_04

West, N. M. (2017). Withstanding our status as outsiders-within: Professional counterspaces for African American women student affairs administrators. *NASPA Journal About Women in Higher Education, 10*(3), 281–300. https://doi.org/10.1080/19407882.2017.1363785

Yosso, T. J. (2005). Whose culture has capital? A critical race theory discussion of community cultural wealth. *Race Ethnicity and Education, 8*(1), 69–91.

CHAPTER 4

PRACTICING AUTHENTICITY IN THE WORKPLACE AS A WOMAN OF COLOR

Janessa Dunn
Vanderbilt University

Authenticity as common practice amongst staff of color in higher education institutions is not existent. To combat the misrepresentation of identity in the workplace, the practice of authenticity must shift from an individualized professional development goal to one that is common practice on all levels of an institution's organizational structure. Implementing a practice of authenticity on the institutional level will support staff of color by offering a safe space for faculty and staff to progress within their fields without forsaking their sense of self.

Red lipstick, Stuart Weitzman pumps, and a heart of gold were staple elements of my grandmother's identity as an educated, Black woman in her community. My grandmother was a direct, polished, and compassionate educator who advocated for young women and men in the Birmingham City School System and Department of Education in Alabama for 33 years. Exhibiting strong faith in advancing the social mobility of people of color

No Ways Tired, pages 31–38

on a large scale in the Jim Crow South, she was a silent soldier who endured perpetual, societal anguish as an educated, Black woman in and out of the classroom; but, she garnered achievement for embracing authenticity as a vital tool for success.

Today, it is not uncommon to compromise one's authenticity in hopes of achieving success in the professional landscape. On the global level in business, many leaders work with constituents who do not share cultural norms and have different expectations for how they should behave (Ibarra, 2015). Oftentimes, this reality forces the perception that leaders should choose between what is expected—and consequently effective—and what feels authentic to them (Ibarra, 2015). The way to combat this perception is utilizing authenticity as a practice in all levels of an organization rather than solely utilizing it as a means for individualized professional development.

As an entry-level professional in the higher education field, specifically in enrollment management, I have the daily privilege to commune with high school students, parents, and guidance counselors, outlining the significant impact that authenticity has on the ability to gain admission and matriculate in college. I preach the value of not losing the essence of their individual goals and passions for the sake of being perceived more favorably among counterparts in the admissions process. Furthermore, I charge students to openly express their unique personalities and passions by reflectively drawing upon their experiences in the classroom, extracurricular activities, and other areas of their livelihood. By doing so, colleges and universities are not only able to identify the students who are a good fit for their institutions, academically and socially; they are also able to be proactive in their approach to support the needs of the students whom they admitted. Thus, if students are not honest in expressing their genuine academic and social identities in their approach to the application process, institutions are at risk of not recognizing the subliminal needs of their students throughout the matriculation process.

In a similar manner, the practice of authenticity in the workplace for faculty and staff of color is equally vital to the recruitment, retention, and progression of faculty and staff of color (Elfman, 2018). If there is no expectation to practice authenticity in the workplace among faculty and staff of color upon entry into their respective institutions, even during the hiring process, institutions are at risk of not recognizing and, consequently, addressing the challenges of faculty and staff of color throughout their tenures at their institutions.

WHAT IS AUTHENTICITY?

According to Merriam-Webster Dictionary, authenticity (n.d.) is the act of being true to one's own personality, spirit, or character. Contrarily, the antonym for authenticity is the act of displaying or portraying a false personality, spirit, or character. Johnson and LaBelle (2017) note that authenticity in relational contexts may be very different from authenticity in teaching (as cited in Flaherty, 2017) or in other educational occupations. Practicing authenticity in the workplace does not require disclosing every single thought and feeling, which is both unrealistic and risky (Ibarra, 2015). On the institutional level, it is important for staff, especially those who seek leadership roles, to develop a personal style that feels right to their personal identity and suits the evolving needs of their respective organizations (Ibarra, 2015).

It is my opinion that practicing authenticity should be evident in enrollment management and student affairs. By setting a precedence of authenticity before students are admitted to an institution, I believe that students are more aware of the expectation of authenticity upon arrival on their college campuses. This practice can be utilized for staff of color as well.

THE CHALLENGE OF PRACTICING AUTHENTICITY AS A WOMAN OF COLOR

As I have successfully sought opportunities to build upon my strengths in leadership, collaboration, and empathy on the professional level, my attempts to exhort my talents were always challenged by an unhealthy need for validation from colleagues, teachers, and other stakeholders in my community. Although I was not overtly vocal about my hidden need for attention and praise, I secretly desired for people to know who I was, why I was important, and why I deserved to have a seat at the table. I needed their approval, not my own. Over time, I learned that my extrinsic need for validation served as a survival mechanism throughout the entirety of my tenure as a student and as an educator. Ultimately, I sacrificed my authenticity for the sake of garnering extrinsic motivation to succeed, academically and professionally.

In high school, my identity as a Black girl was often in conflict, academically and socially. At home, I was comfortable with expressing my personality, character, and identity openly among friends and family; however, in school—which was predominantly White—I often hid attributes of my cultural heritage by changing the way I talked, dressed, and my community of friends to be perceived as the perfect, model student of color.

Because the culture of my environment did not overtly support authenticity on the school level—and therefore, perpetuated the notion that the "White way" of doing things was the unilateral, acceptable way of doing things—I cultivated a flawed view of my identity as a Black student and as a member of a racial group with a rich cultural history. For example, as one of very few Black students in the classroom, I was often called upon to give an overgeneralized, abbreviated history lesson of the triumphs and tribulations of Black people in America—which reduced the teaching of Black history to the recitations of a teenager who was inadequately armed with the knowledge base to speak on the subject and too timid to advocate for more instruction on Black history by teachers.

Unfortunately, unilateral pressure to assimilate into a dominant culture was also practiced by members of the Black community, specifically in the way in which we talk and how our hair is styled. As a scholar, my ability to speak articulately in the classroom was challenged by the label of not being "Black enough" in the lunchroom amongst a group of my Black classmates. For young Black girls, hair has the power to dictate how they are treated, and in turn, how they feel about themselves (Thompson, 2008). At the age of nine, I was diagnosed with Alopecia Areata, an autoimmune disease that inhibits the growth of hair follicles, leading to baldness (National Alopecia Areata Foundation, 2018). This condition altered the way I was treated in the classroom, on the soccer field, and among my friends and family. Although my parents spent thousands of dollars on custom wigs and dermatological scalp injections to induce hair growth, bullying by other Black girls persevered. In essence, I was isolated by other Black girls because of a cultural norm that views hair as a symbol of status in the Black community (Thompson, 2008).

These juxtaposed experiences directly affect the way I approach professional and personal relationships today. For staff of color, it is crucial to consider the power and value of listening to and appreciating the narratives of colleagues, students, and community members to gain a broader understanding of the stratified experiences of fellow people of color. It is my opinion that a person's narrative identity, or life story, has a vital role in understanding how one performs and progresses in the professional landscape, especially for those whose professional roles are directly or closely aligned with their sense of purpose.

Narrative identity is described as "a person's internalized and evolving life story, [which integrates] the reconstructed past and imagined future to provide life with some degree of unity and purpose" (McAdams & McLean, 2013, para. 1). Consequently, for staff of color whose narrative identities are in alignment with their professions, it is important for institutions to recognize key areas in which they can be proactive in embracing the narrative identities of staff of color during the recruitment and hiring process and incorporating authenticity as a common practice in all areas of the institution to retain staff of color.

To be clear, the practice of listening to the experiences of staff of color does not mean that staff of color should perpetually memorialize trials and triumphs that were experienced in the past. Rephrasing the definition of narrative identity by Dan McAdams and Kate McLean (2013), Herminia

Ibarra (2015) suggests that leaders within an organization should be wary of allowing past experiences to be the steering force in approaching new situations; rather, one should have confidence in their personal story and embrace how their story evolves into a new narrative over time. Hypothetically, it would be ineffective for me to utilize my experience of being bullied as young girl as the extrapolative argument for my not being chosen for a promotion that was awarded to a fellow Black woman who perceivably has a more "suitable" hairstyle. She simply may have been a more skilled fit for the position. Instead, I can utilize my previous experiences to serve as a daily motivation tool to address behavior that diminishes the identities, talents, and passions of Black women because of the type of hairstyles they choose to wear in the workplace and in other settings.

Furthermore, it is important for staff to recognize that identity—and therefore authenticity—is neither unidirectional nor unidimensional. Recently, I met with a high school classmate to reflect on our similar narratives of surviving and thriving as Black women who were perpetually challenged inside and outside of the classroom to be perfect, model students of color. We discussed how our dual perceptions of identity as high school students—"not Black enough" and "too White"—have impacted our professional and personal journeys as young adults. Ultimately, we discovered that the act of altering aspects of our identities as Black women in the classroom—the way we talked and dressed—was not performed out of malice or arrogance; it was a form of survival to perform at our highest potential in an environment that did not truly understand how our identities influenced success. Unfortunately, we were not taught how to be authentic and successful simultaneously in a White-dominated culture.

HOW DOES AUTHENTICITY AFFECT THE RETENTION AND SUCCESS OF STAFF OF COLOR?

Delving more deeply into understanding the narratives of staff of color helps institutions address the mannerisms of staff of color that are deeply seeded in a mechanism for survival rather than authenticity. The stakes are higher for staff of color to advocate for higher levels of authenticity in the workplace. It is my opinion that staff of color who are key leaders and stakeholders on their college campuses should lead by example in practicing authenticity to model that authenticity and success do not have to be mutually exclusive for them to succeed in the academy. More so, all constituents at institutions—administrators, faculty, and staff—should actively support an organizational structure that provides a safe space for staff of color to progress within their respective organizations with authenticity.

Ultimately, obstacles in the workplace that pressure staff of color to assimilate to the dominant culture directly affect their success. If staff of color feel like they cannot "show up" in the workplace in an authentic way, this limits their ability to connect with their students (Johnson & LaBelle, 2017); and, it can limit opportunities for leadership development (Ibarra, 2015). Because identities are outwardly displayed in today's landscape of hyper-connectivity and social media, how we present ourselves as people beyond our leadership roles, with quirks and broader interests, has become an essential pillar of leadership (Ibarra, 2018). Furthermore, curating a persona that is not genuine, or false, can clash with our private sense of self (Ibarra, 2015). From personal experience, the act of practicing a false representation of self is mentally, emotionally, and physically exhausting; and, it is unsustainable for a long-term career in education that is founded upon cultivating a safe space for students to be authentic in their daily lifestyles and careers. As Harvey-Wingfield (2017) suggests, institutions must create safe spaces for faculty and staff of color to succeed in all levels of an institution's organizational structure.

HOW CAN HIGHER EDUCATION PROFESSIONALS MOVE THE NEEDLE FORWARD IN SUPPORTING A CULTURE OF AUTHENTICITY AMONG COLLEAGUES AND CONSTITUENTS?

As an alternative way to connect with staff of color, I strongly believe community members on college campuses should actively pursue empathy as part of their everyday practice. Social scientist Brené Brown (2015), whose current research focuses on authentic leadership and wholeheartedness in families, schools, and organizations, describes empathy in the following way:

> The most powerful tool of compassion, is an emotional skill that allows us to respond to others in a meaningful, caring way. Empathy is the ability to understand what someone is experiencing and to reflect that understanding. [It is] important to note here that empathy is understanding what someone is feeling, not feeling it for them. If someone is lonely, empathy [does not] require us to feel lonely, too, only to reach back into our own experience with loneliness so we can understand and connect. (pp. 155–156)

In the academy, the practice of empathy may be perceived as a soft measure to address organizational concerns for a critical mass of individuals. However, for staff of color, it is crucial for universities to understand how narrative identities are intertwined within the professional roles of people of color. The way to do so is by practicing empathy.

CONCLUSION

While society had not recognized the magnanimity of my grandmother's identity as a Black woman in the classroom, she decided not to allow the pressures of assimilating to a White-dominated culture to stand in the way of creating a space for the positive trajectory of her students' lives. Similarly, I have chosen to highlight my metaphorical Stuart Weitzman pumps and red lipstick to signify my authentic, fierce role as an educator—but not without confronting challenges.

Although my grandmother was a "Wonder Woman" to many, she confronted me in my early school years about how society perceives educated Black women. The anecdotal lessons of "working twice as hard to get half as much" and ensuring that my teachers always perceived me as a perfect, model student of color were well-intended; but they also impeded my ability to embrace authenticity in my professional life.

If institutions incorporate authenticity as a practice in the recruitment and hiring process as well as throughout the tenures of staff of color at their respective institutions, everyone wins—students, faculty, staff, and the institution at-large. If authenticity is practiced daily, entry-level professionals will be better equipped to support the needs of their students, colleagues, and the missions of their institutions.

REFERENCES

Authenticity (n.d.). In *Merriam-Webster Dictionary.* Retrieved from https://www.merriam-webster.com/dictionary/authenticity

Brown, B. (2015). *Rising strong: How the ability to reset transforms the way we live, love, parent, and lead.* New York, NY: Random House.

Elfman, L. (2018, April 15). Black academics urged to retain authenticity, respect, vision. *Diverse: Issues in Higher Education.* Retrieved from http://diverseeducation.com/article/114358/

Flaherty, C. (2017, May 25). Study on students and 'authenticity' in classroom. *Inside Higher Ed.* Retrieved from https://www.insidehighered.com/quicktakes/2017/05/26/study-students-and-authenticity-classroom

Harvey Wingfield, A. (2017, September 9). Faculty of color and the changing university. *Inside Higher Ed.* Retrieved from https://www.insidehighered.com/advice/2016/09/09/more-faculty-color-can-and-should-be-top-ranks-universities-essay

Ibarra, H. (2015, January–February). The authenticity paradox. *Harvard Business Review.* Retrieved from https://hbr.org/2015/01/the-authenticity-paradox

Johnson, Z. D., & LaBelle, S. (2017). An examination of teacher authenticity in the college classroom. *Communication Education, 66*(4), 423-439. https://doi.org/10.1080/03634523.2017.1324167

McAdams, D. P., & McLean, K. C. (2013). Narrative identity [Abstract]. *SAGE Journals, 22*(3), 233–238. https://doi.org/10.1177/0963721413475622

National Alopecia Areata Foundation. (2018). *What you need to know about the different types of alopecia areata. National Alopecia Areata Foundation.* Retrieved from https://www.naaf.org/alopecia-areata/types-of-alopecia-areata

Thompson, C. (2008). Black women and identity: What's hair got to do with it? *Politics and Performativity, 22*(1). Retrieved from http://hdl.handle.net/2027/spo.ark5583.0022.105

CHAPTER 5

STAYING WOKE

Strategies for Impacting Diverse Student Populations When Not Directly Working With Them

Jarett D. Haley
University of Michigan

Staff of color can sometimes find it difficult to positively affect the experiences of diverse students when their positions do not require them to work with these students directly. This situation can consequently pose a threat for institutions to retain these professionals when it becomes apparent to staff that they are not having the impact they imagined upon entering the field of student affairs. Thus, this chapter will present strategies for effectively reconciling one's passion for social justice and supporting diverse students, with the lack of opportunity to do so that is occasionally presented by specific student affairs functional areas or an institution's student demographics.

Many prospective student affairs professionals who identify as people of color choose to enter the field, and even where to apply to graduate programs, based on their commitment to social justice work and a passion for

No Ways Tired, pages 39–48
Copyright © 2019 by Information Age Publishing
All rights of reproduction in any form reserved.

supporting students from traditionally marginalized groups (Linder & Simmons, 2015). When they eventually enter the field, however, they are occasionally presented with potentially problematic circumstances given their goals. Not only do they often end up working at predominantly White institutions (PWIs), which is not an inherent issue, but also sometimes find themselves in roles that may not seem designed to have the type of impact these zealous, new professionals would ideally hope to have. For instance, there are some functional areas within student affairs in which the day-to-day responsibilities do not necessitate exposure to social justice work or work specifically related to diverse student populations (e.g., career services, student conduct/behavioral case management). Moreover, there is a potential for this lack of desired impact to occur for staff in areas that would presumably entail this type of exposure (e.g., on-campus housing, student activities). Staff of color working in student activities at PWIs, for example, with few diverse students could potentially find themselves lamenting the dearth of opportunities to work with the populations that interest them on their campuses. Staff members in these situations need to find ways to still engage with the types of student communities and issues that brought them to this field despite not being directly tied to them through their work responsibilities. This issue is particularly crucial given that PWIs tend to experience difficulties retaining staff of color (Jackson & Flowers, 2003) and staff can easily become disenchanted with their institutions and the field of student affairs if they believe they are not having the impact they initially envisioned (Marshall, Gardner, Hughes, & Lowery, 2016).

Luckily, however, there are various ways for staff to impact the specific student populations they are passionate about even when their job responsibilities do not require them to do so. As a student affairs professional of color working in career services at a PWI, I have personally had to find ways to assist these types of students and have thankfully, been able to do so by (a) collaborating on projects across functional areas, (b) continuing my education, (c) supporting student-led initiatives, and (d) volunteering. This chapter will elucidate these strategies by providing examples of their successful implementation from my personal experiences, along with scholarly support for their usage. In addition, this chapter will serve as a call to action for supervisors and institutions as they can encourage staff to take advantage of these opportunities outside of their immediate work responsibilities and help facilitate the process.

INTENTIONAL COLLABORATION

In my experience, one of the most intuitive and effective ways to work with diverse student populations when not exposed to them on a regular basis is to collaborate with colleagues on campus who are. For many institutions, these individuals are often staff members working in campus cultural centers. Diverse students derive numerous benefits from spending time in these centers, including a sense of community and safety (McDowell & Higbee, 2014; Patton, 2006). Thus, working with staff members who operate within these spaces offers a great opportunity to connect with students who may not feel as comfortable in other areas of campus as they do in the cultural center. Meeting with students in spaces on campus where they feel most at ease has worked for me, specifically, through my collaborative work with my institution's Black cultural center (BCC) and intercultural center (IC).

For instance, over the past two years I have conducted several workshops at the BCC to help students prepare for various networking events being held on campus. Through these workshops, I have assisted many students who, prior to meeting me, had never interacted with anyone at the career services (CS) office. Given the negative treatment Black students have reported experiencing at PWIs by individuals across campus including administrators (Suarez-Balcazar, Orellana-Damacela, Portillo, Rowan, & Andrews-Guillen, 2003), this lack of exposure to another predominantly White administrative office was not too surprising. However, seeing this play out within the context of my own work made me realize how crucial my partnership with the BCC truly was to the success of these students. My goal of positively impacting diverse students was furthered through this joint effort, which as Aguinis et al., (2016) notes can be a common result of collaboration.

In addition to supporting my goals, my collaborative work has given me access to some of the tacit, institutional knowledge possessed by my colleagues. This type of knowledge is often necessary for sustainable success within an institution and my work with the IC exemplifies this necessity quite well. During the 2016–2017 academic year, the assistant director of the IC and I developed a series of workshops designed to help diverse students begin to establish cultural and social capital during their time in college. Initially, despite feeling confident in my ability to run the workshops, I was nevertheless perturbed by the task given my lack of experience marketing events to specific student demographics (the BCC handled the marketing for networking workshops). Nevertheless, my concerns were quickly assuaged by my colleague in the IC who possessed a wealth of knowledge and experience with successfully attracting our institution's diverse students to events. My colleague has since moved on to another college; however, I still possess the knowledge he shared with me and have used it in my efforts to promote workshops to students along with sharing this information with other colleagues. My work continues to benefit immensely from tacit knowledge sharing and I attribute this success to my experience with my former colleague in the IC. Moreover, I have noticed over time that my most effective collaborations have come from working with colleagues who similarly not only possess tacit knowledge and are willing to share it, but who can also operationalize this often taken for granted information.

SUPPORTING COLLEAGUES THROUGH SELF-DIRECTED LEARNING

Acquiring knowledge from outside of one's institution (e.g., research, best practices) can also assist student affairs professionals of color in their work to support diverse students. This idea is endorsed by scholars and professional associations arguing that to meet the needs of an ever-changing student population, student affairs professionals must continue to seek out sources for learning and skill development (ACPA: College Student Educators International, 2010; Haley, Jaeger, Hawes, & Johnson, 2015). Some of the most popular sources of edification in student affairs are the annual professional development conferences hosted by organizations like the National Association of Colleges and Employers (NACE) and the National Association for Student Personnel Administrators (NASPA). Conferences can be great places to learn about successful programs and network with colleagues at different institutions. However, despite their benefits and prevalence in the field, the actual knowledge gained and skills developed by conference attendees are often quite nebulous (Haley et al., 2015). I recall one instance after attending an annual career services-focused conference when I struggled to identify discernible takeaways that I could use for my work with students. Despite participating in sessions that were advertised as offering innovative strategies for supporting diverse students, for example, there were often very few ideas mentioned that were not already being implemented in my office. In my experience, conferences have not been the most effective or efficient way to gain specific knowledge and skills since attendees can only control the sessions they attend, but not the content of sessions. In contrast, similar concerns are not as apparent with more self-directed learning (e.g., personally chosen courses, one's own reading) since the individual tends to have full (or at least more) autonomy over the information presented. I have had this type of experience through my reading and the courses I have taken as a professional, which has not only informed my work with students but also the work of my colleagues.

Through self-directed learning, I have remained aware of contemporary issues facing diverse students and used this information to support the program planning of my colleagues. Learning by way of self-direction is not a new concept in student affairs as scholars have shown its use over the years by mid-level managers, for instance, to develop their skills in supervision (Nichols & Baumgartner, 2016). Similarly, from personal experience, I can attest to its benefits for entry-level professionals. For example, during our office's annual staff retreat, my fellow counselors often ask me about new concepts or research I have been exposed to, knowing that I am studying current issues in higher education in my coursework. Given that much of the courses I have chosen to take (e.g., Theories of Diversity in Higher Education) and things I read on my own deal with supporting diverse students, the information I share with them frequently revolves around strategies for working with these students. For instance, there was one moment when we were discussing the programming needs of first-generation and low-income students and my insight helped focus the conversation. We were specifically contemplating the ways in which our programming related to this population could be improved when at one point, I drew the group's attention to two of the main concerns facing these students: a lack of financial resources and a sense of belonging at their institutions (Katrevich & Aruguete, 2017; Nuñez, 2011). This information assisted in organizing our thoughts by showing the group what they were already doing to address these issues and what things needed to be considered to begin attending to them further.

JUDICIOUSLY STANDING BEHIND STUDENT ACTIVISTS

On their own, students often attempt to address issues afflicting diverse peers on campus as well as issues with larger social implications by relying on the power of the protest. Although seen as antithetical to the goals of higher education at one point, student activism is now widely regarded by scholars and student affairs professionals as essential to student development (ACPA: College Student Educators International, 2010; Bernardo & Baranovich, 2016; Biddix, Somers, & Polman, 2009; Hamrick, 1998). Some of the specific learning outcomes for students include, but are not limited to, an appreciation for civic engagement, the development of personal values, and the cultivation of a sense of community on campus (Biddix et al., 2009). Given the various benefits students gain from their efforts, institutions should not only encourage and facilitate activism among students (Bernardo & Baranovich, 2016; Biddix et al., 2009), but also among the wider campus community, including student affairs staff. In addition to promoting learning outcomes, activism would also give staff members who identify with the students or issues being protested an opportunity to show their solidarity with the students (which could help staff members feel part of the larger campus community too).

Although, even with the approval of one's institution, some staff members may still find it difficult to support student activism as actively as they would like given the issues frequently presented by their "dual roles as institutional representatives and educators" (Hamrick, 1998, p. 457). How does one aid student activists while also demonstrating to students the importance of respecting the institution's perspective? This conflict can be particularly arduous to manage for entry-level professionals as they often have yet to fully understand their responsibilities to the institution. Nevertheless, despite the difficulty, it is possible to reconcile these competing interests. One way I have found helpful to do so is to provide an equal level of involvement in activism-related efforts to that of my more experienced colleagues.

A great example of this strategy is my participation in our college's fossil fuel divestment movement (not directly related to diverse students but still relevant). As a proponent of environmental sustainability, I immediately wanted to show my support to our students' divestment initiative when I began working at my institution. However, I was unsure of how to tactfully approach this situation given our college's sentiment on the issue (i.e., they were not divesting from fossil fuels). Fortunately, I eventually found a campus group of fellow staff and faculty members who also opposed investing in fossil fuels and promoted the students' efforts. I was then able to see, through their participation, what an appropriate amount of involvement would be for me (e.g., I have a fossil fuel divestment poster hanging outside of my office door). Therefore, if staff of color find themselves in a similar situation at their institutions, it would be in their interest to seek out like-minded colleagues to determine what degree of involvement in student activism is typical on their campus.

DONATING YOUR TIME WITH THE HELP OF YOUR INSTITUTION

Lastly, I believe it is incumbent upon higher education institutions to encourage staff of color to take advantage of volunteering opportunities. The benefits gained from volunteering by employees, organizations, and students are well documented (Bell, 2007; Gray, 2010; Longenecker, Beard, & Scazzero, 2013). Through their formal volunteer programs (e.g., service learning), higher education institutions and for-profit companies, for example, often promote the numerous volunteer hours contributed by their students and employees to increase their standing within their communities and garner greater brand recognition (Gray, 2010; Longenecker et al., 2013). On the other hand, personal development is a more frequently cited outcome of volunteering for students and employees (Bell, 2007; Gray, 2010; Longenecker et al., 2013). In addition, volunteering can result in distinct benefits for specific groups of employees. Some people believe volunteering can be an effective tool for increasing the community engagement of employees who identify as part of a traditionally marginalized group and specifically, increase their engagement with the communities most salient to their identities (Gray, 2010).

Through my personal experience with volunteering, I derived all the aforementioned benefits and also discovered a different way to support students that many staff members may not consider. For example, I currently volunteer with a research group studying the teaching and learning process in higher education. Although the group has broad aims for the potential impact of the research, I have begun to think about some of the specific questions raised as they relate to the diverse student groups that interest me. For instance, because of membership in this group, I developed an interest in studying the pedagogical practices best suited for promoting persistence in college for Black males. This experience shows not only how volunteering can support a student affairs professional's desire to impact diverse student populations, but also how staff members can potentially benefit from taking advantage of nontraditional volunteer opportunities (e.g., research).

For student affairs professionals of color to fully enjoy these benefits, their institutions need to promote volunteering as a worthwhile activity for staff members (and not just students). Institutional support for staff volunteering is vital for many reasons, including the fact that many staff members of color may be unaware of the benefits of volunteering due to a lack of cultural capital (Harflett, 2015). For instance, some have suggested that participation in volunteer activities can be understood through cultural preferences and practices (i.e., cultural capital) that are often tied to one's ethnicity and class (Harflett, 2015). Thus, staff members could be (dis)inclined to volunteer based on their background. Furthermore, staff of color may have more to gain through volunteering due to their race and ethnicity than other employees, like a sense of empowerment and positive effects to their physical health (Tang, Copeland, & Wexler, 2012). In the end, if institutions are truly committed to developing their staff of color, particularly entry-level staff, then they should display the same level of enthusiasm and support for staff volunteering as they do for student volunteering.

STUDENT AFFAIRS STAFF AND RESEARCH

Before ending this section, I believe the idea of staff members taking advantage of nontraditional volunteer opportunities, and specifically research, warrants further consideration. Just as faculty often hope to positively affect specific communities with their research, many staff members wish for a similar type of influence in their direct work with students. However, many staff members, and specifically entry-level staff, could also achieve their desired impact by participating in research. While student affairs work gives staff the opportunity to support individual students on a campus, the number of students that staff can potentially impact by engaging in scholarly research is nearly limitless. Institutions around the world will have access to one's findings and will be able to implement suggested interventions on their campuses.

Additionally, although staff are sometimes presented with circumstances that may initially appear to preclude them from engaging in research, such as their lack of knowledge about research opportunities or their physical location, they can still find ways to get involved. For instance, many professors in higher education and student affairs graduate programs actively recruit volunteers to join their research teams or projects. Although they typically look for current graduate students, many professors also welcome professional staff who are interested in their work. For instance, I was one of several student affairs staff members participating in my research group. Furthermore, depending on the type of research project, location won't necessarily limit involvement as team meetings and work related to the project could be done virtually.

CONCLUSION

The strategies I have discussed in this chapter, based on my personal experience, show how student affairs professionals of color can support the student populations that interest them while not working with them directly. Those strategies include: (a) collaborating on projects across functional areas, (b) continuing one's education, (c) supporting student-led initiatives, and (d) volunteering. However, while I did implement them successfully, these strategies may not be possible or appropriate for everyone to use on their specific campus. I, therefore, suggest utilizing the suggested strategies when applicable in concert with a myriad of other strategies collected from various resources (e.g., other student affairs professionals, research, networking). The more strategies student affairs professionals use, and specifically professionals of color, the better their chances of positively impacting diverse student communities.

Supervisors of professionals of color in student affairs and their institutions can also play a role in helping staff have their desired impact and, in some instances, they can be the deciding factor. To support this claim, I will share that all the strategies I implemented were either facilitated through my supervisor/institution or had the potential to be supported by my supervisor/institution. For instance, as an entry-level staff member, I'm not sure that I would have had the courage to reach out to my BCC and IC colleagues for collaborative work if my supervisor had not made the initial suggestion and introductions. In addition, I might have experienced less difficulty with supporting student activism if I knew about the appropriate level of staff participation sooner. Given that retention for student affairs staff is a serious issue in higher education (Jackson & Flowers, 2003; Marshall et al., 2016), supervisors and institutions must be more proactive if they are to have any success in addressing it. One way to do this is to support the efforts of staff members as they attempt to positively affect the experiences of diverse students.

REFERENCES

ACPA: College Student Educators International. (2010). *ACPA/NASPA professional competency areas for student affairs practitioners.* Washington, DC: Authors.

Aguinis, H., Davis, G. F., Detert, J. R., Glynn, M. A., Jackson, S. E., Kochan, T., . . . Sutcliffe K. M. (2016). Using organizational science research to address U.S. federal agencies' management & labor needs. *Behavioral Science & Policy, 2*(2), 67–76.

Bell, C. (2007). Using employee volunteering programs to develop leadership skills. *Development and Learning in Organizations: An International Journal, 21*(1), 6–8. https://doi.org/10.1108/14777280710717407

Bernardo, M. A., & Baranovich, D. (2016). Dissent by design: Fostering student activism in higher education through a case study of student affairs in a public university in the Philippines. *Journal of College Student Development, 57*(2), 197–209. https://doi.org/10.1353/csd.2016.0024

Biddix, J. P., Somers, P. A., & Polman, J. L. (2009). Protest reconsidered: Identifying democratic and civic engagement learning outcomes. *Innovative Higher Education, 34*(3), 133–147. https://doi.org/10.1007/s10755-009-9101-8

Gray, B. (2010). The rise of voluntary work in higher education and corporate social responsibility in business: Perspectives of students and graduate employees. *Journal of Academic Ethics, 8*(2), 95–109. https://doi.org/10.1007/s10805-010-9105-0

Haley, K., Jaeger, A., Hawes, C., & Johnson, J. (2015). Going beyond conference registration: Creating intentional professional development for student affairs educators. *Journal of Student Affairs Research and Practice, 52*(3), 313–326. https://doi.org/10.1080/19496591.2015.1050034

Hamrick, F. A. (1998). Democratic citizenship and student activism. *Journal of College Student Development, 39*(5), 449–459.

Harflett, N. (2015). Bringing them with personal interests: The role of cultural capital in explaining who volunteers. *Voluntary Sector Review, 6*(1), 3–19. https://doi.org/10.1332/204080515x14241616081344

Jackson, J. F. L., & Flowers, L. A. (2003). Retaining African American student affairs administrators: Voices from the field. *College Student Affairs Journal, 22*(2), 125–136.

Katrevich, A. V., & Aruguete, M. S. (2017). Recognizing challenges and predicting success in first-generation university students. *Journal of STEM Education, 18*(2), 40–44.

Linder, C., & Simmons, C. W. (2015). Career and program choice of students of color in student affairs programs. *Journal of Student Affairs Research and Practice, 52*(4), 414–426. https://doi.org/10.1080/19496591.2015.1081601

Longenecker, C. O., Beard, S., & Scazzero, J. A. (2012). What about the workers? The workforce benefits of corporate volunteer programs. *Development and Learning in Organizations: An International Journal, 27*(1), 9–12. https://doi.org/10.1108/14777281311291213

Marshall, S. M., Gardner, M. M., Hughes, C., & Lowery, U. (2016). Attrition from student affairs: Perspectives from those who exited the profession. *Journal of Student Affairs Research and Practice, 53*(2), 146–159. https://doi.org/10.1080/19496591.2016.1147359

McDowell, A. M., & Higbee, J. L. (2014). Responding to the concerns of student cultural groups: Redesigning spaces for cultural centers. *Contemporary Issues in Education Research (CIER), 7*(3), 227–236. https://doi.org/10.19030/cier.v7i3.8643

Nichols, K. N., & Baumgartner, L. M. (2016). Midlevel managers' supervisory learning journeys. *College Student Affairs Journal, 34*(2), 61–74. https://doi.org/10.1353/csj.2016.0012

Nuñez, A. (2011). Counterspaces and connections in college transitions: First-generation Latino students perspectives on Chicano studies. *Journal of College Student Development, 52*(6), 639–655. https://doi.org/10.1353/csd.2011.0077

Patton, L. D. (2006). Black culture centers: Still central to student learning. *About Campus, 11*(2), 2–8. https://doi.org/10.1002/abc.160

Suarez-Balcazar, Y., Orellana-Damacela, L., Portillo, N., Rowan, J. M., & Andrews-Guillen, C. (2003). Experiences of differential treatment among college students of color. *The Journal of Higher Education, 74*(4), 428–444. https://doi.org/10.1353/jhe.2003.0026

Tang, F., Copeland, V. C., & Wexler, S. (2012). Racial differences in volunteer engagement by older adults: An empowerment perspective. *Social Work Research, 36*(2), 89–100. https://doi.org/10.1093/swr/svs009

CHAPTER 6

THE BLACK EXPERIENCE

Terrance I. Harris
Oregon State University

Navigating through higher education while maintaining professionalism is a challenge, especially being an African American male. This chapter explores my journey thus far through higher education. My experiences began as an undergraduate and continued to graduate school after 3 years of working in corporate America to my career in student affairs. Support and mentorship are key components to my success as a student affairs professional in addition to me taking risks. I offer suggestions to new professionals from my professional perspective to help them navigate their journey as they begin their career in student affairs.

THE BEGINNING

Growing up, my family never spoke about higher education. Education in our house meant that you would get a high school diploma. My mother received her diploma and became a beautician and my father dropped out in the ninth grade. None of my siblings went to college and even the mention of college to my mother engendered an automatic negative response.

No Ways Tired, pages 49–58
Copyright © 2019 by Information Age Publishing
All rights of reproduction in any form reserved.

I was determined and motivated to travel a different path than my parents or siblings, to make it big and provide financial support to my mother in the future. The only route I knew at that point in life was to get a college degree. First generation college students, such as myself, are pioneers for their families; it takes a major leap of faith to alter the picture.

Choosing a college was an interesting experience for me. I yearned for the Black college experience and really wanted to attend a Historical Black College or University (HBCU); however, lack of scholarships (and also being rejected then accepted by an institution) hindered me from attending an HBCU. Televisions shows like "A Different World" and "The Cosby Show," which showed Black students like myself going to school, joining Black fraternities and sororities, and having so much pride were relatable and just really made me feel like I would be at home in that setting. However, I attended Western Kentucky University (WKU), a predominantly White institution, where I had an amazing experience.

While at WKU, I was fortunate to meet some awesome people with a few becoming my mentors. One of them was Dr. Monica Burke, who at the time worked in the Office of Diversity Programs (ODP) and guided me into the field of student affairs. Dr. Burke, along with others in ODP, kept students of color engaged in campus activities and helped shape my college experience. Additionally, I was heavily involved in several diverse activities: keeper of Exchequer for Kappa Alpha Psi Fraternity Incorporated; held membership with the Amazing Tones of Joy Gospel Choir; lecture chair for the Campus Activities Board; as well as Alpha Kappa Psi Business Fraternity. Looking back, I do not know how I managed to juggle so many groups while being a student. Consequently, I now find myself advising my mentees not to overbook themselves, but to gain meaningful experiences while being engaged on campus.

Navigating through higher education is a challenge, especially being an African American male and gay, on top of not having a mentor to guide me. The wrong choice in a mentor or making friends may result in a negative perception from peers. Furthermore, being a bisexual or queer (GBQ) person of color brings about unforeseen challenges, especially to many Black males. Washington and Wall (2010) described the dilemma Black males face when choosing which identity they should show on any day. When choosing a mentor, this quandary played a factor as I pondered whom I could trust and would not judge my lifestyle. In the end, my mentors had a good pulse on my personality, positioned me in spaces to be successful, and encouraged me to become involved in various campus activities. There were moments, however, I felt that parts of my identity needed to be suppressed, especially in highly toxic masculinity areas like a fraternity for example.

Like many student affair professionals, I had not realized that being part of those student organizations would lead to a career in higher education.

My goal was to get a degree in business marketing education and teach key-boarding to ninth and tenth graders. However, my capstone project brought forth a spark to my work in student programming I created and produced a fashion show entitled "WKU Rip Da Runway" in 2007, (which is still in existence in 2018), and was a collaborative effort with the Merchandise and Textile Department, the Black Student Alliance, and the Campus Activities Board. Consequently, I always encourage students to "leave a mark"—create something of quality that will continue to go on or be remembered years after they leave campus. Involvement in these organizations can lead to invitations from senior-level administrators to serve on various advisory boards and committees within the university. Harper (2008) highlighted the significance of Black male achievers fostering relationships with senior level administrators. Those relationships support connections, internship opportunities, career references, and essentially help mentorship evolve. This continuance is the epitome of building a legacy and in hindsight, set the path for my journey in student affairs. Mentors like Dr. Burke, Creston Lynch, Howard Bailey, Nayasha Farrior, and many others gave me a foundational understanding on how to interact with my students. It was their check-ins, casual conversations, and guidance that navigated me through my undergraduate experience. Knowing how helpful their interactions were for me, I knew only but to try that formula with my students and it has worked. As Harper (2008) eluded, it is imperative for mentors, administrators, faculty to be an influence in our students' path through college, especially those of color (particularly Blacks). I do not believe everyone needs to mentor students; but I do believe wisdom in moments is generally welcomed, especially in spaces where people of color are not shown in great numbers.

My journey toward student affairs continued after graduating from WKU in May 2007. I began to work at the United States Census Bureau. At that time, I thought I landed a great job in my hometown of Louisville, Kentucky, making a nice hourly wage (for what I later learned was for 100 hours per month). I then obtained a second job in a law firm pushing mail and making copies to support my income; neither job related to my degree or required a college degree. Feeling frustrated and defeated, I did not know what to do but knew my potential was greater than my circumstances and I refused to settle. Still well connected to my mentors at WKU, I reached back out to Dr. Burke for advice on career opportunities. She encouraged me to attend graduate school and study higher education although I was initially adamant about not going. Dr. Burke explained the types of positions within higher education that caught my attention and provided information on several great programs for me to apply. I always enjoyed planning events and after some deliberation, campus activities and multicultural affairs soon became my focus leading me to a master's degree in higher education at the University of North Texas (UNT).

GROWING PAINS

My graduate experience at UNT was so dynamic and inspirational. The amount of support I received prepared our "no hort" platform to be successful in any area of student affairs. This moment was also when I was truly on my own and began to learn more about myself. For example, in Dr. Bush's social justice class, I learned about the "model of Black identity development" by Cross and Fhagen-Smith (Vandiver, Fhagen-Smith, Cokley, Cross, & Worrell, 2001) and really acquired an understanding of identity development, especially in correlation to race. I began to examine my own identity while also evolving within that identity.

My first day on campus, I met Dantrayl Smith who really helped connect me to a network throughout campus and the Black Graduate Student Association which was a great experience for me and a part of my success at UNT. As Astin (1999) discussed, student involvement relates to the amount of energy invested. Being involved in activities opens the door for academic success, which includes interactions with faculty/staff as well as encourages and provides resources for students. For example, one of my favorite professors, Dr. Bonita Jacobs, asked how I was doing personally and being frank, I told her I was looking for a job after being on campus for a month. She replies, "Just one second" and made a call to the union director; then turns to me and says, "You will receive an email by the end of the day." Her care and effort led to my position as a graduate assistant within the university programming office to advise the university program council. I will never forget her sincere support in helping me get my first job. She is now the president of the University of North Georgia and we continue to stay connected. One small conversation opened the door to the first major step in my career. Accordingly, I encourage graduate students to build sustainable communication and relationships with faculty and staff.

As humans, we desire a sense of belonging and a way to foster a community where we are a part of a group with strong in-group bonds where participants share similar traits (Park, 2008). On a college campus where students are entering a new and unknown environment, finding social belonging takes on more meaning. For students of color at predominantly White institutions they became part of a subordinate environment, so involvement and social belongingness is paramount. They are likely to experience stress related to such an environment because of their group(s) identity is stigmatized and becomes the target of discrimination and prejudice (Carter, 2007). Being part of support network, which can include peers, faculty, and staff, can play a significant role in enhancing their development, sustaining their well-being, and buffering some of the negative effects associated with being a student of color in a predominantly White environment.

An important component of my social belonging began when I met one of my best friends through my graduate program, GeColby Youngblood. The stress of school, finances, organizational commitments, and personal life issues lingered but our friendship and continuous encouragement kept us going. We also built relationships with faculty and staff who soon became our mentors. Once a month, Dantrayl would gather all the Black faculty, staff, and graduate students at the university for a men's lunch. These lunches were an opportunity for us all to vent, discuss current events, provide wisdom, and just enjoy each other's company. As Schwitzer, Griffin, Ancis, and Thomas' (1999) research suggested, social adjustment at predominately White institutions can be influenced by eliminating a hurdle of approaching faculty and recognizing the effects of faculty familiarity. When students of color have familiarity with faculty, their ambivalence dissipates as they feel a sense of similarity to the faculty member based on race or gender or both. In the lunch setting, students felt more comfortable communicating with professors that shared commonalities such as race and gender so, a support network was established. Although I sometimes complained about attending the Black men lunches, I later understood the importance and relevance they had in that space on that campus. To be around Black men in esteemed positions at the institution was inspiring to me and having a Black vice president at the university as a mentor laid the foundation for my goal in higher education to eventually become a vice president of student affairs one day.

SEARCHING FOR TRUTH

For my first job search, which lasted 8 months, I participated in the major job searches (i.e., TPE, AC3) as encouraged by mentors within my graduate program. During the process, I consistently practiced my elevator speech and had my résumé destroyed, reconstructed, and then destroyed again several times to ensure my qualifications stood out. In my first on-campus interview, I felt good about my performance as I was crisp on my knowledge about student development theory and had ideas on how to implement some amazing initiatives. Despite my preparation and solid performance in multiple interviews, I was always "a great candidate" but never "the best fit." Frustrated and slightly depressed, I began to question my existence in the field; yet, I was not going to quit as my faith was too strong. After being on the search for a job for 6 months, I decided to broaden my scope and eventually had an interview with Stetson University for their assistant director of health promotion position. Ideally, I did not want to go into health promotion although my previous graduate assistantship was in that role. My graduate assistant position in student health and wellness at UNT was not a position I initially desired, but I would later recognize that my work was a key to my success. First, I was pushed to work and think outside of my comfort zone and second, the position provided me with new, requisite knowledge. In my interview at Stetson, I decided to make a bold move with an interactive presentation focusing on various risky sexual behaviors (including words such as frottage, digital penetration, and analingus with protection). The staff laughed the entire time, appeared to love it, and the next morning I woke up to a phone call from the director, offering me the position in the Wellness and Recreation Department at Stetson University. To new professionals, my biggest advice is never give up! This suggestion does not mean you should settle for anything, but it does mean know your worth and keep fighting. Keep looking for that open door and be grateful for the ones that closed. I learned that some institutions that told me "no" was protection and a blessing from God as there was drama and chaos that I did not see.

TRANSITIONS

Woo is my highest theme on the StrengthsQuest and I certainly won others over at Stetson University through my dynamic presentation, personality, and what I later realized—being Black. I was the only African American male professional staff member in my department and in the entire division. This circumstance not only was a learning curve for me to retain knowledge of the position, but to navigate through a lack of mentorship, advisement, or connection of individuals who resembled me. In addition, I had to adapt quickly as the Black students soon saw me as a resource and mentor. When Black students would enter my office, and see the awards I had received as an undergraduate student, mementos with influential people such as Dr. Maya Angelou and Jeff Johnson, and pictures with my fraternity brothers, they would stare for a while and follow up with questions about my experience in college. Reverting to my graduate school days, I began to think of the model of Black identity development theory, which became very salient in my role at Stetson. Sector 4 (low race salience) and Sector 5 (encounter) were focus points of our students' development as there were not many activities that exemplified Black culture (e.g., the National Pan-Hellenic Council [NPHC]). Many students had no prior knowledge of such activities while others were yearning for those types of activities. At the right time, I was asked to provide advice and support to Stetson's Greek Life office to bring an NPHC organization to campus and eventually, was asked to advise Sigma Gamma Rho Sorority Incorporated. It was a challenge to reassure those young women that they were beautiful and to build a foundation for other groups to come, especially since predominantly White fraternities and sororities would utter racial slurs and engage in offensive acts toward the women.

In addition to educating students, there were moments I had to enlighten my team on issues specifically associated with Blacks and other minorities. For example, on professional development days, I discussed models like "Black identity development" (Cross & Fhagen-Smith, 2001) and White identity development (Helms, 1993) since my colleagues possessed limited knowledge or experience with social identity development models. Ultimately, such responsibilities began to weigh me down; however, for the first time in my career, I had no one of color to confide in as a mentor. My mentors, except for Dr. Burke, had suddenly become ghost once I started at Stetson, which was very difficult for me. Having no one nearby to turn to, my supervisor with whom I had a good relationship, suggested I build a relationship with our vice resident of student affairs. What she failed to understand was the importance for me to have Black male mentorship. In addition, my supervisor encouraged me, with my vice president's support, to begin looking at other positions that fulfilled my desires. Initially, I did not know how to take that feedback, so I asked her directly about the intent behind her suggestion. Later, after our discussion, I understood that she wanted to support me although I did not agree totally with the approach. Looking back, I appreciated the gesture my supervisor made to support the advancement of my career. Often, one questions the motives of supervisors or higher administrators when suggestions to look elsewhere are made.

On July 4, 2014, my life came to a dramatic halt when my father died suddenly in his home from an apparent heart attack. After I took a week off to plan and attend his services, I decided that this moment was a major turning point in my life. Although my father and I had a strained relationship that healed as I got older, I realized the impact I made on his life and how his death affected me. From that moment, I spent the next year and half planning to leave Stetson and find myself. Again, I went on countless interviews with various institutions across the country with thoughts of "not the best fit" replaying in my mind. During this time, I was highly encouraged, twice, to apply for a position at Oregon State University (OSU). My gut reaction was "no" and I wondered who would support me there, especially when I lacked support and mentorship in Florida. Finally, I gave in just to see what would happen and after a successful phone interview, I was offered an on-campus interview. I figured at least there is a free trip to Oregon, a place I may never visit again so let me see what this position is all about. The support and resources available on the campus amazed me and I began to reconsider. One thing I learned through this process is that when one door closes, another one will open to put you closer to your destiny.

NEW BEGINNINGS

In January 2016, I began my role as director of the Lonnie B. Harris Black Cultural Center (LBHBCC), one of seven cultural resource centers at OSU. Leaving Stetson was harder than I thought, it was my first job and I had made some amazing friends and my résumé grew substantially, a benefit of wearing multiple hats working at a small private institution. I now entered a new environment that is predominantly White and not much "seasoning" (people of color) anywhere. My role as director of the LBHBCC is to support the Black community through events, discussions, academic achievements, and mentorship. I find myself in the "bicultural" stage of Black identity development (Cross & Fhagen-Smith, 2001). Having the support yet giving pieces of my identity away to make the small Black population feel supported as well as others. Mentorship of students and staff is more important now because I know how it is to have a lack of support and no one to provide insight. Although I miss my students at Stetson, I am so grateful to be at OSU and know that my presence is necessary. My load is heavy but the resources and benefits are unlimited. Since I arrived at OSU, I have spoken to many groups, traveled the world, and built bridges between the university and community partners. I know that in this environment, I can move toward my full potential in every area of life and have unlimited growth.

WORDS OF WISDOM FOR GRADUATE STUDENTS AND NEW PROFESSIONALS

To the younger and current entry-level professionals in student affairs, my advice to you is as follows:

1. Live your best life professionally and personally.
2. Find someone on campus whom you can confide in but be okay if those individuals do not resemble you. Although I preferred a Black mentor, especially on campus, I did have some amazing colleagues who had my best interest at heart but were not Black.
3. If you attend professional conferences, seek out some mid-level professionals willing to be your career mentor. When I was a graduate student, I developed relationships with seasoned professionals who were heading in the direction I wanted to go. Seek those who have similar values, vision, and aspirations.
4. I would encourage new professionals to be open and authentic. Students know when you are not being real and that determines how they will react and receive you. Be willing to be vulnerable. We ask students to do this, yet we avoid certain aspects of going to that

space. I am not encouraging anyone to divulge their entire lives, but share some things that may help a student to feel included and supported. Over the past 8 years, I have developed great relationships with my students because I kept it real. Regardless of the situation, I always provide some wisdom, advice, opinion, or story to help them think about their next move. You never know how your story may influence the next person. There are students who do not have anyone providing guidance or support in their lives and student affairs professionals can offer that guidance and support to them.

5. Mentorship is essential for us as professionals just as much as it is for students. Mentoring focuses on more than providing support for another person's future as emphasis should also be on the development of your skills in academics, personal lives, and career.

6. Overall, continue to be you and be willing to evolve. No matter what setting, always be yourself. I have grown professionally, mentally, spiritually, intellectually but at the end of the day, I remain Terrance. As Dr. Martin Luther King Jr. emphasized "If you can't fly then run, if you can't run then walk, if you can't walk then crawl, but whatever you do you have to keep moving forward." Never let a professional, student, or administrator hinder you from the greatness you imprint on others' lives. Be you and be great.

REFERENCES

Astin, A. W. (1999). Student involvement: A developmental theory for higher education. *Journal of College Student Development, 40*(5), 518–529.

Carter, R. T. (2007). Racism and psychological and emotional injury: Recognizing and assessing race-based traumatic stress. *The Counseling Psychologist, 35*, 13–105. https://doi.org/10.1177/0011000006292033

Cross, W. E., & Fhagen-Smith, P. (2001). Patterns of African American identity development: A life span perspective. In C. L. Wijeyesinghe & B. W. Jackson III (Eds.), *New Perspectives on Racial Identity Development* (pp. 243–268). New York, NY: New York University Press.

Harper, S. R. (2008). Realizing the intended outcomes of *Brown:* High-achieving African American male undergraduates and social capital. *American Behavioral Scientist, 51*(7), 1030–1053.

Helms, J. E. (1993). *Black and White racial identity: Theory, research, and practice.* Westport, CT: Praeger.

Park, J. (2008). Race and the Greek system in the 21st century: Centering the voices of Asian American women. *NASPA Journal, 45*(1), 103–132.

Schwitzer, A. M., Griffin, O. T., Ancis, J. R., & Thomas, C. R. (1999). Social adjustment experiences of African American college students. *Journal of Counseling & Development, 77*, 189–197. https://doi.org/10.1002/j.1556-6676.1999.tb02439.x

Vandiver, B. J., Fhagen-Smith, P. E., Cokley, K. O., Cross, W. E. Jr., & Worrell, F. C. (2001). Cross's Nigrescence model: From theory to scale to theory. *Journal of Multicultural Counseling and Development, 29*(3), 174–200.

Washington, J., & Wall, V. A. (2010). African American gay men: Another challenge for the academy. In M. J. Cuyhet (Ed.), *African American men in college* (pp. 174–188). San Francisco, CA: Jossey-Bass.

CHAPTER 7

I ACCIDENTALLY DISCOVERED MY PURPOSE

Tassany C. Henderson
Vanderbilt University

This chapter focuses on the road to self-discovery. The author explains how through self-reflection and careful consideration, specific skills can be developed. Additionally, the author shares how resourcefulness, flexibility, networking, and developing a team of mentors can lead toward a successful career in student affairs. The author will convey a message of determination, motivation, and encouragement to the reader. Lastly, the author will discuss the importance of developing skills that can help the reader determine their purpose in life.

I remember it like it was yesterday. I was four years old and wearing my white cap and gown with my diploma in hand. I had just graduated from preschool and was moving to kindergarten. I was so excited, but not for the obvious reasons. In my mind, since I graduated, that meant it was time for me to get a job. Although I had the concept right, I was a few years too early. Even as a young child, I understood the notion that gaining an education was the gateway to obtaining a career. Throughout my journey, which included transitions and pivotal moments, I endured sleepless nights wondering which route was best for me. During those times, I relied on my family, friends, and my faith for guidance. Even more so, I developed four skills that have guided me along my journey from college student to student affairs professional.

SENIOR YEAR

The day was Monday, August 16, 2004, the first day of my senior year in high school. I attended a small school with grades from fifth to 12th grade. Our school consisted of a very close community that totaled around 900 students. All of us were on a college track, so it was clear that education did not end at graduation. During my senior year, I completed college applications, composed personal statements, and requested letters of recommendation for scholarships. As a first-generation college student (FGCS), defined as "students where neither parent attended or completed college" (University of Southern California, para. 1), I was completely on my own regarding my journey to higher education. My parents held blue collar jobs but always preached the importance of seeking higher education; however, other than encouragement, there was not too much more my parents could offer. In fact, my mother paid a company $100 to show us how to complete the Free Application for Federal Student Aid (FAFSA). Although it appeared to be common sense, it was never explained to us that there was not a fee required to complete the application. With the lack of knowledge from my parents, I was forced to find answers in other ways.

My senior year in high school taught me my first lesson—the importance of being resourceful; embodying the ability to make lemonade out of lemons. It has proven to be instrumental to my success repeatedly. For me, passion, dedication, and motivation could turn any negative situation into a positive one. Anna Solley and Naomi Story (2015) authored an article outlining several leadership competencies, including resourcefulness, that lead to the development of "transformational leaders" (p. 3). These competencies were adopted by the American Association for Community Colleges (AACC) and reviewed by the National Council for Black American Affairs (NCBAA). Upon reviewing the AACC report in detail, NCBAA study participants highlighted the ability to be resourceful was a trait or "soft skill" that leaders should possess (Solley & Story, 2015). Relatedly, my interpretation of being resourceful is not to have limitless resources, but the ability to accomplish your goal with what you have at your disposal. My mother was always known for saying she could "make a dollar holler!" which meant that she could make the best out of what she had. A person can accomplish anything if they have an unlimited amount of resources, but it takes grit and perseverance to persist when there are limited means available.

COLLEGE DAYS

A little more than a year later, on Saturday, August 20, 2005, I moved into my dormitory at Middle Tennessee State University (MTSU). My mind was filled with mixed emotions; however, I did not have any feelings or thoughts of fear. The reality was that statistically, as an African American female from a low-income household, I was not expected to succeed. There are a growing number of researchers who suggest that minority students living in urban areas from low socioeconomic backgrounds are less likely to enroll in institutions of higher education once they graduate from high school (Rall, 2016). In academia, this is called the "summer melt," a phenomenon that occurs when "college-intending high school graduates encounter barriers to college enrollment" (Rall, 2016, p. 462). Additionally, this experience can occur even when students have "...been accepted to at least one college, applied for financial aid, and submitted applications for additional scholarships" (Rall, 2016, p. 462). I made it through the summer and was ready for what college had to offer. It was my opinion that things would be different because I was different. In my mind, I had the next four years mapped out. I had no intention of switching my major like so many of my peers did. In fact, in 2005, it was estimated that close to 80% of students changed majors at least once before they completed their degree (Chen, 2005). Consequently, my environment limited my exposure to an expansive selection of career options and for the most part, my day-to-day circle exposed me to teachers, factory workers, and other blue collar careers. I also relied heavily on the thoughts of others and what they believed I should pursue. My options included becoming an attorney, physician, or teacher. I chose to major in political science and become an attorney.

I completed my first two and a half years of college and managed to maintain a B average. My plans were still to pursue a graduate degree in law but I slowly began to realize that I did not enjoy my coursework. Despite my disenchantment with my program, I was very engaged with many co-curricular activities within the Center for Student Involvement and Leadership (CSIL) at MTSU. I had no idea my involvement would change the outlook on my purpose in life. By the time I completed my junior year in college, I was completely fed up with my major. Enrolling in summer courses, I had the opportunity to graduate early and being so close to graduation, changing my major was out of the question. I knew I wasn't going to law school and I did not want to teach. I decided to speak with the vice president for student affairs at MTSU, Dr. Debra Sells, and during our meeting, I explained how my desire to pursue law ended and I was unsure what career was in my future. She reminded me about how involved I was in the student affairs community at MTSU and more specifically, CSIL. She asked me if I had considered pursuing a graduate degree at MTSU in administration and supervision with a higher education concentration. Up until that moment, it never dawned on me that all the people who helped me in college were indeed professionals. I knew my professors were on a career path, but I never viewed all the student affairs professionals in the same light. In that moment, my future was born.

My undergraduate years taught me my second lesson—in addition to being resourceful, being flexible helped me prevail through many difficult personal and professional situations. Although the plan when I began my undergraduate studies was to become an attorney, things changed and it was up to me to change with them. Rowley (1997) wrote that being versatile allows someone to "maximize opportunities for future development and flexibility to change in response to external circumstances" (p. 6). Throughout my life, my faith impressed upon me the ability to bend like a palm tree. For me, that meant that although the winds in life may blow and I might bend, I could weather the storm, stand tall, and not break. You will not be able to serve yourself or your students if you are broken. You must have the ability to be versatile and the flexibility to adjust when necessary.

THE REAL WORLD

I took Dr. Sells' advice and began my master's of education degree in Fall 2009 at MTSU and graduated in Fall 2010. Although I questioned my decision, my faith and my relationship with God allowed me to trust the decision. Graduate school was completely different from my undergraduate experience, as I was absolutely in love with the material. Everything about my program was awesome and I took advantage of every lecture, guest speaker, and reading assignment. Along the way, I got married and there seemed to be endless things to celebrate. Then, there was the brick wall. Once I began the job search in my career, I realized these positions were not so easy to secure. For some institutions, I managed to get an interview but I would often hear that I was overqualified because of my graduate degree.

It was in a very strange place. Having my master's degree without professional experience made it difficult to find a position. The reality was in the world of higher education, obtaining a position is about who you know and who knows you! I knew the importance of networking and how it was needed to begin my career in higher education. Eventually, I found a position at Cumberland University in the Office of Admissions. I did not know many people in the industry but there was one person I had a few courses with who worked there. I reached out to her, she mentioned my name to her director, and the rest was history. I was given an interview, I rocked it, and was offered the position. A little over a year, my husband and I had our daughter and later, I moved on to work at Nashville State Community College. While there, I learned both good and not so good leadership skills that would prepare me for a future leadership position. In 2016, I began pursuing my doctoral degree at Trevecca Nazarene University in leadership and professional practice.

During my doctoral program, I was given an assignment to create my own personal board of directors. Little did I realize that this was something that I had been doing since my undergraduate studies. We were required to identify a group of mentors who could provide career/professional suggestions and feedback. Additionally, we were encouraged to seek out people in senior level positions who were doing what we aspired to do. Each step of the way, I gathered people to serve on my board of directors. I managed to meet prospective mentors in meetings, conferences, luncheons, classes, and many other settings. Although my team is inclusive of higher education professionals, they have become trusted friends of mine as well. Because of these experiences, I believe that an individual should take a step out on faith and introduce themselves to someone they do not know.

There are two takeaways. First, everyone needs a trustworthy team of mentors. Second, networking has been a very effective skill that has assisted in my professional development. Kram (1988) confirmed that the career mentoring process can bring about efficiency in job performance, cultivating political capital, establishing collegial relationship, fostering job satisfaction, and nurturing organizational commitment. Accordingly, it is essential to develop a core group of trusted individuals, no matter if you are new to higher education or a seasoned professional.

TYING IT ALL TOGETHER

As an African American female raised in a low-socioeconomic household, I was expected to fail. Society's depiction of me was meant to make me feel inadequate or beneath my Caucasian counterparts. Fortunately for me, I was determined to pursue a less traveled path. Life, thus far, has not taken me in the direction I chose more than a decade ago. Now as a professional woman, I know my journey's direction. Instead of being oppressed by what I am, I use my experiences, good and bad, as a platform to help others. My life experiences helped me to sharpen my skills. The adversity I encountered allowed me to develop my resourcefulness. Without change, I would not know how to be flexible. Lastly, conflict and confusion have shown me the importance of networking and establishing a support system. During my days of uncertainty,

I rely heavily on my family, friends, and my faith. Along the way, I knew that while I was unsure of the journey, my steps were divinely ordered. I would not change my experiences because they have helped me to develop a skill set that has served me well and allowed me to discover my purpose. I encourage all new and entry-level professionals of color to not focus on the twists and turns in life, but to evaluate what they have learned from each of them. Nothing in life is constant or guaranteed; life is ever-changing. I challenge each person to look within and discover their purpose.

REFERENCES

Chen, X. (2005). *First generation students in postsecondary education: A look at their college transcripts.* Washington DC: U.S. Department of Education, National Center for Education Statistics.

Kram, K. E. (1988). *Mentoring at work: Developing relationships in organizational life.* Glenview, IL: Scott, Foresman, and Company.

Rall, R. M. (2016). Forgotten students in a transitional summer: Low-income racial/ethnic minority students experience the summer melt. *The Journal of Negro Education, 85*(4), 462–479.

Rowley, J. (1997). Academic leaders: Made or born? *Industrial and Commercial Training, 29*(3), 78–84.

Solley, A., & Story, N. O. (2015, February 9). Diversity & leadership in the 21st century. *The Hispanic Outlook in Higher Education, 25*, 21–24.

University of Southern California. (2017). *First-generation at USC.* Retrieved from http://dornsife.usc.edu/first-generation-college-students-at-usc/

CHAPTER 8

THE "I" IN THE IVORY TOWER

On Fighting "I"ndividualism
Through the Collective "We"

Brooke Huynh
The University of Rhode Island

In this chapter, I will share the experiences I have as a graduate student and person of color in the College Student Personnel Program at the University of Rhode Island. Starting with my time working professionally in the student activities office at a small liberal arts college, I witnessed how the lack of visibility of Asian American students contributed to the model minority myth. Furthermore, I discuss the structures in higher education that create isolation among individuals of color. As a result, I speak about the microaggressions I experienced in my first year as a graduate student. My chapter ends with a call for action towards unity and a "we" culture among people of color despite being in an American educational system built on individualism and meritocracy.

My name is Ngan Ha Ly Huynh. I am in my final year of the college student personnel graduate program, under the Department of Human Development and Family Studies, at the University of Rhode Island. I received my

No Ways Tired, pages 65–74
Copyright © 2019 by Information Age Publishing
All rights of reproduction in any form reserved.

undergraduate degree in history and gender studies in 2015 from Mount Holyoke College and then worked at a small liberal arts college for 2 years in their student programs office. In English, my name means *river of money* and *milky way*. My family settled in Portland, Maine in 1980 through a family based immigration program. A pseudonym, Artist College, has been chosen to as a way to leave out identifying information about this institution.

My preferred name, Brooke, stems from the name of a brook in Da Nang, Vietnam that my father fished in before he immigrated to the United States. My name was given to me as an homage to my Vietnamese culture. As I grew older, I distanced myself from my Vietnamese heritage and embraced the privilege that I have as the first in my family to be born in the United States. Today, I am a proud, strong, American woman, who has a complicated relationship with her American identity.

American citizenship is a privilege that influences how I view my name and myself. While attending Mount Holyoke College, I focused my undergraduate work on interrogating my privilege as a citizen of the United States. As I studied my ancestry, I started to understand my history and its relationship to the Vietnam War, which still has a significant impact on my family identity today. Vietnamese culture values kinship and family, honoring ancestors, and preserving history. These values stand in sharp contrast to the American values of individualism and meritocracy. Dominant cultures, oppressive structures, and White supremacy are entities that reinforce "I" and erase Asian American realities. By focusing on the "we," which include family values, community building, and collective action, we can develop a common identity as oppressed people of color.

I began to appreciate the collective power of "we" when I began my professional journey into student affairs at Artist College in 2015. It is a commonly held misconception that Asian Americans are more successful than other racial groups. In academia, this phenomenon is known as the "model minority myth" (Kwon, 2010). I witnessed this pervasive misconception in action while working at Artist College and it has directly shaped how I view my work in student affairs ever since. Artist College's mission is to provide a unique college experience by subverting the common narratives of traditional college education. There are no majors at Artist College. Instead, students find their own academic pathway. When students are encouraged to create their own academic pathways, dominant ideologies of individualism are reinforced (Sensoy & DiAngelo, 2012). This focus on "I" can lead to isolation and further divisiveness. This thought was especially apparent among students of color, who chose to take the path of "I" instead of "we." As a person of color working at a predominantly White institution, I observed a significant amount of resources allocated for Black and Latinx students while Asian students were left behind on the assumption that they, the "model minority," had everything they needed. Accordingly,

Asian American identity groups did not receive the same recognition as other identity groups. Resources to support Asian American populations were therefore minimal, but funding for other larger identity groups were a priority. The lack of resources, programs, and support dedicated to Asian American students likely stemmed, at least partly, from the model minority myth. When Asian Americans are viewed as successful, it is easy to divert resources to other campus needs.

I also witnessed firsthand at Artist College "the oppression Olympics," the concept of competition between minority groups to determine who is "most oppressed" (Hancock, 2011). Students of color would regularly compete for resources and fight amongst each other by asking, "Which identity group is the most oppressed?" "Who belongs in the cultural center?" "Whose needs are more urgent than mine?" This competition created a hierarchy where groups who were the most vocal about their oppression gained the most attention. Artist College's individualistic culture, in part, contributed to this competitive, "me first" narrative. Dissention and divisions among student organizations of color kept them from communicating, coexisting, and resisting dominant forms of oppression collectively as "we." Students of color were too focused on "I" and their specific needs as individual racial and ethnic groups.

Witnessing identity politics among student organizations of color gave me the space to think about the divisions among people of color and the lack of coalition building between marginalized groups. I continued to ponder the matrix of oppression in higher education and the divisiveness of "I." Although most individuals I have encountered during my career have had little difficulty identifying their own victimization within a major system of oppression, they typically fail to see how their own thoughts and actions uphold someone else's oppression. I understand that though I will never understand the experiences of other identity groups, but by placing minority groups on the hierarchical continuum, no room is left for a collectivist "we" approach to understanding oppression and the common marginalities that people of color face. Though systems of oppression will occur in diverse and varying ways, there must be collectivity among people of color rather than a division. By bringing together a diverse range of experiences among people of color, we begin to strengthen our voice in numbers and thereby, increasing the visibility of people of color and the everyday oppressions we face. By empathizing with other people's experiences, we create space for dialogue regarding our differences, make meaning for ourselves, and subvert the dominant narrative of divisiveness and isolation. We cannot use the individualistic language of "I" as the primary tool to deconstruct oppression within the institutions that were not built for us. Instead, "we" must collaborate and use our differences to strengthen the cause against systematic oppression in higher education.

THE MODEL MINORITY MYTH AND ASIAN IDENTITIES
IN HIGHER EDUCATION

The erasure of Asian American experiences depresses available resources based on the myth that "Asian Americans are doing just fine." Therefore, the contemporary Vietnamese-American experience is rarely talked about in higher education. This lack of attention partly results from the United States' political emphasis on individualism and colorblind ideologies that lead to the erasure of people of color (Sensoy & DiAngelo, 2012). The model minority myth furthers the erasure of Asian American realities and perpetuates a widespread notion that Asian Americans have overcome racial discrimination and are more successful than other people of color (Suzuki, 2002). The model minority myth has often been used strategically by opponents of affirmative action to support the myth of meritocracy (Museus & Kiang, 2009; Sensoy & DiAngelo, 2012). Proponents against affirmative action say that discrimination does not exist and point to the educational success of Asian Americans as proof that America is "post-racial" (Covarrubias, 2014). Yet, there are vast educational disparities among ethnic groups who often get homogenized within the Asian racial label. In fact, research shows that Southeast Asian American students graduate college at rates significantly lower than other East and South Asian American identities (Museus & Kiang, 2009). The model minority myth has also contributed to why there is a lack of literature on Asian American populations (Museus & Kiang, 2009).

The research on the Vietnamese American experience is even more sparse. Specifically, there is little research on Asian American faculty and administrators, which adds to the invisibility of Asian Americans as a group in higher education. As a graduate student, I have witnessed the invisibility and misrepresentation of Asian American people in curriculum. For instance, the most known social identity theory, Kim's Asian American Identity Development model, highlights the social and psychosocial experiences of being an Asian American minority in the United States (Patton, Renn, Guido, & Quaye, 2017). Kim's Model, like many racial identity models, fails to acknowledge the differences in racial and ethnic compositions within the Asian American population. It is inaccurate to assume that Asian American populations will move through phases of understanding of their own Asian American development because there are cultural, generational, and social values that construct understandings of Asian American identities. Asian American identity models based on Western notions of "individualistic" identity development, without understanding the "we"—that is the collaborative, community, and familial relations central to many Asian American communities—are inaccurate and serve to erase cultural realities rather than clearly articulating cultural experiences.

THE PEDAGOGY OF THE OPPRESSED

I have come to see notions of individualism—and the focus on "I"—to be the tool of the oppressor. Lorde (1984) wrote that the need for unity is often misunderstood for homogeneity. To build a coalition of "we," we must develop a collective identity, a collective of difference. Freire (1992) described the power of collective action amidst an oppressor's attempts to take power over minority communities. In the initial stage of struggle, the oppressed are so crippled by their own reality of oppression that they fail to understand how their actions are incongruent with the oppressor (Friere, 1992). Friere (1992) also wrote about the individualistic qualities of the oppressor—they follow a set of rules that are driven by the dominant quest for power. The quest for power can only exist if there are other people who do not have power. Without considering the matrix of oppression that we all inhibit, we cannot liberate ourselves from the oppressor. We must recognize the causes of oppression so that we can overcome it. However, combating oppression is not something we can do on our own. Resistance takes collective power, unity, and navigating across difference to fight the oppressor. Both Friere and Lorde call for motivational change—the collaborative engagement among the marginalized to reclaim the master's toolbox.

In the context of higher education, it can be easy to accept and be complicit in the hierarchical power structure. However, as the oppressor wants to keep the power it holds to maintain systems of oppression, one way the oppressed can take back their power is to build relationships. In my work, I try to build relationships and coalitions with as many colleagues as I can. Through relationship building, I am strengthening the collective power within my community, which helps me to build a stronger voice in the fight against oppressive structures in higher education. With more individuals who are fired up and are ready to participate in the call to action, there becomes more visibility. Systematic structures previously upheld such as the lack of visibility of people of color, the burden that people of color have in being overworked and underpaid, and the microaggressions that people of color face every day, can be undone if we change the institution that created those structures in the first place. It is this collective power that moves our higher education system from a culture of "I"—that is the separation and divisiveness among groups—into a culture of "we," a place of collectivist difference.

DEFINING A COLLECTIVIST COMMUNITY (OR LACK THEREOF) AT URI

It did not take long for me to notice how many students were learning the fundamentals of social justice for the first time, whereas I spent most of my college career teaching, learning, and unpacking my own marginalities and privileges. Having gone to Mount Holyoke College, where advocacy for marginalized individuals was a pillar of the university's mission to having worked at Artist College where the curriculum was focused on honoring a student's unique contributions to the world, to University of Rhode Island (URI) where I was alone, both within and outside of the classroom. At the time, it did not seem as if there were other allies of color who could support me. I was alone because my existence was a threat against the comfort that White students had been afforded their entire life. In the first weeks of my career at URI, I encountered many macroaggressions from my peers:

"We are all the same."

"I used to teach in the city and most of the students were Hispanic, they were often loud."

"All lives matter because my family created their livelihood out of being cops in the ghetto."

"I'm not racist because my boyfriend is Black."

These stark comments, edited slightly to preserve anonymity, are all examples of the everyday encounters I heard as a student of color in my graduate program.

Hearing these comments forced me to turn inward; it is not my job as a person of color to educate White peers about racism. How do I channel moments of frustration, anger, and resentment? How do I process my own emotions, trauma, and genuine outrage at the micro (and sometimes macro) aggressions? How can I shift my energy into something productive that would move us towards liberation? Ultimately, during the moments I worked to call out inappropriate behavior, my White peers would be defensive, shift blame, and speak about how they were triggered by *my* comments. For students just beginning to understand the fundamentals of social justice, my calling attention to oppressive behavior led to feelings of White fragility. I witnessed that when racism was brought up and my White peers felt uncomfortable, they blamed me, the "angry woman of color" who triggered the discontent in the room (DiAngelo, 2006).

Robin DiAngelo's work around Whiteness and racism shows there is literature to describe the phenomenon I experienced in the classroom. DiAngelo (2006) speaks about how many students are oblivious to the structural inequalities in society that are deeply embedded within our American school system. Individuality is an American value. Individuality allows White people to appear "diverse in their experiences" without having to understand race as a paradigm (DiAngelo, 2006). When people of color suggest that White people are oblivious to race, the exchanges lead to a defensiveness, a privilege only given to Whites. Racial comfort becomes not expected, but demanded (DiAngelo, 2006). There is ample evidence of how White institutions perpetuate and maintain power, but the question *is what do we do* about it?

The answer to this question is complicated, daunting, and oftentimes feels impossible to unearth. However, in overcoming my own perceptions, thoughts, and feelings about what it means to work in higher education as a person of color, I found a way out of my own isolation with an agenda in mind—find places where I could facilitate a "we" culture. I created a space where students could come as their full authentic selves and we worked co-collaboratively to take back the master's tools that divided us. During the spring semester, I worked with the associate director of diversity initiatives at the University of Rhode Island Graduate School. Together, we created a curriculum open to all graduate students that would provide opportunities for dialogue on issues of social justice.

My experiences observing macroaggressions in the classroom inspired me to create a multicultural education curriculum for other graduate students where I brought together individuals from a variety of disciplines to build a collective community. During the program, students developed the language and frameworks needed to build collective change. I saw the real and tangible transformative experience that participation gave students through the evaluations and self-assessments that students completed. In teaching and helping students grapple with how salient and non-salient identities influence how we frame and understand race and systems of oppression, I began to create a "we" community where we can face complex issues of inequality together. Upon completion of the program, we were still connected. I still maintain connections with individuals in the program through sharing teaching resources and offering support to other graduate students to fight against the system that divided us.

Upon completion of the professional development program, I was elected to become president of the graduate student union. Unions are a space built upon collective power. There is more bargaining power when there are more people and numbers. My position as president allows me to push for active change, to help build a "we" culture. A culture where we, the marginalized, get to take back the master's tools. Right now, we are working on a collective bargaining strategy to help develop more funding avenues to recruit students of color at the graduate level. We are advocating for higher raises so that graduate students can have a livable wage while they attend the University of Rhode Island. We are advocating for more faculty of color, staff of color, and more opportunities to work with faculty unions. Though I am building and advocating for change in a visible way, I am not doing this alone. In the fall semester of 2017, I felt isolated. I felt as if my voice was silenced due to the macroaggressions I faced in the classroom. I noticed the lack of representation of people of color within and outside of the classroom and I expressed frustration and anger. However, after much self-reflection and interrogating my own educational privilege, I used my privilege and knowledge to create change. My privilege as an educated, strong woman from an elite private institution allowed me the opportunity to have the pedagogy, curriculum building skills, and the ability to teach and mentor others in multicultural education. The experiences I have as a student of color in a student affairs program led me to think about ways I could build a "we" culture full of difference and collective power.

LESSONS LEARNED: NAVIGATING IDENTITY AS A PERSON OF COLOR AT PREDOMINANTLY WHITE INSTITUTIONS

I end my chapter with a few takeaways from what I learned as a Vietnamese American person of color. As people of color who work at predominantly White institutions, it can be easy to work in isolation. We are focused on surviving. We evaluate choices to sustain our being such as, "Which diversity committee do I sit on?" or "How do I support my students and do my job?" The truth is as people of color, we cannot combat racism alone. The institutions of higher education were not built for people of color and institutions are going to continue to force us to fight amongst each other for resources and opportunities. When we are fighting against each other, we do not bring together our collective power, which is what the oppressor wants.

Secondly, I urge student affairs professionals to think about their privileges as well as their marginalization. We cannot understand the fabric of oppression without understanding the privileges we are afforded. For me, I had to look inward to understand my own educational privilege. I went to a liberal, private women's college where I had the opportunity to make mistakes, unpack my own identity, and learn social justice language. Though higher education is a hierarchical system not built for us, are we complicit in the oppression that could hurt others? Many people of color can articulate clearly their own marginalities but oftentimes, the challenge lies in understanding our privileges too. Among my own social justice communities, I have seen a phenomenon called, "call out culture." Call outs are a public act of addressing someone else's comments or words that are perceived to be oppressive especially within the progressive community (Ahmad, 2015). The act of "calling out" is a form of policing; the person enacting the call out gets to decide who is in the community and who is out (Ahmad, 2015). In addition, the person engaging in the call out often has privilege of their own—the knowledge and expertise that they have demonstrated by addressing someone else's perceived oppressive language choice. Social justice language is always changing and it is impossible to keep up with every word and phrase used in our field. There is a disposability politics to call out culture, where instead of "calling in" the act of addressing privately the thoughts or actions of an individual, the public act is meant to shame or address the oppressive behavior without providing a chance for dialogue (Ahmad, 2015). Calling out culture becomes toxic because the person who is wrong, who usually has a marginalized identity, is immediately identified as an outsider in the community. The divisive nature of calling out creates a culture of alienation, an insider/outsider dichotomy, and further creates divisiveness among people of color.

Lastly, it may seem like fighting against systematic oppression is impossible. And it is. But that does not mean we should give up. I am urging my fellow student affairs professionals of color to find networks in which they can build a "we" culture. This system could include building a "we" culture through curriculum building or bringing together other people of color in a union or even joining a professional organization for people of color in higher education. We cannot be complicit in fighting against our own oppressions. When we define ourselves only in the "I," we do not leave room for the collective understanding of "we" rooted in marginality and difference.

REFERENCES

Ahmad, A. (2015, March 2). *A note on call-out culture.* Retrieved from https://briar patchmagazine.com/articles/view/a-note-on-call-out-culture

Covarrubias, A., & Liou, D. D. (2014). Asian American education and income attainment in the era of post-racial America. *Teachers College Record, 116*(6). Retrieved from https://www.tcrecord.org/content.asp?contentid=17279

DiAngelo, R. J. (2006). My class didn't trump my race: Using oppression to face privilege. *Multicultural Perspectives, 8*(1), 51–56.

DiAngelo, R., & Sensoy, Ö. (2010). "OK, I get it! Now tell me how to do it!": Why we can't just tell you how to do critical multicultural education. *Multicultural Perspectives, 12*(2), 97–102. https://doi.org/10.1080/15210960.2010.481199

Freire, P. (1993). *Pedagogy of the oppressed* (20th Anniversary ed.). New York, NY: Continuum.

Hancock, A. (2011). *Solidarity politics for millennials: A guide to ending the oppression Olympics.* New York, NY: Macmillan.

Kwon, H., & Au, W. (2010). Model minority myth. In E. W.-C. Chen & G. J. Yoo (Eds.), *Encyclopedia of Asian American issues today* (pp. 221–230). Santa Barbara, CA: ABC-CLIO LLC.

Lorde, A. (1984). *Sister outsider: Essays and speeches.* Trumansburg, NY: Crossing Press.

Museus, S. D. (2008). The model minority and the inferior minority myths: Understanding stereotypes and their implications for student learning. *About Campus, 13*(3), 2–8.

Museus, S. D., & Kiang, P. N. (2009). Deconstructing the model minority myth and how it contributes to the invisible minority reality in higher education research. *New Directions for Institutional Research, 2009*(142), 5–15. https://doi .org/10.1002/ir.292

Patton, L. D., Renn, K. A., Guido, F. M., & Quaye, S. J. (2016). *Student development in college: Theory, research, and practice* (2nd ed.). San Francisco, CA: Wiley.

Sensoy, O., & DiAngelo, R. (2017). *Is everyone really equal?: An introduction to key concepts in social justice education.* New York, NY: Teachers College Press.

U.S. Department of Education. (2017). *Digest of Education Statistics, 2017.* Washington, DC: National Center for Education Statistics. Retrieved from https:// nces.ed.gov/programs/digest/d17/tables/dt17_306.10.asp?current=yes

CHAPTER 9

UPLIFTING COUNTER-NARRATIVES

The Experiences of Women of Color Student Affairs Professionals Teaching in White Classrooms

Nadeeka Karunaratne
University of California–Los Angeles

Carol Huang
University of California–Santa Barbara

Ginny Jones Boss
Kennesaw State University

Aliya Beavers
University of Houston–Clear Lake

No Ways Tired, pages 75–86
Copyright © 2019 by Information Age Publishing
All rights of reproduction in any form reserved.

This chapter examines the experiences and strategies of new and entry-level women of color student affairs professionals as they navigated teaching in predominantly and historically White college classrooms. Utilizing a critical race feminist framework, we share counter-narratives of the authors and participants who engaged in a collaborative autoethnographic study on the topic. We highlight challenges regarding teaching that stem from the specific intersections of our gender, race, and professional identities. We uplift the voices of women of color by sharing the lessons we learned. Finally, we provide recommendations to support new and entry-level women of color student affairs professionals as they navigate their multiple identities to promote student learning, practice self-care, and thrive.

As women of color, we experience microaggressions on a regular basis at the intersections of our racial, gender, and other marginalized identities. These experiences of racism, sexism, and other forms of oppression do not remain isolated to our personal lives—they impact our work as student affairs professionals. For women of color student affairs professionals who work in predominantly or historically White colleges, issues and dynamics related to intersectional identities are often magnified. Additionally, for new and entry-level student affairs practitioners who also teach, the challenges they face in the classroom may be new and unexplored, requiring additional support in their navigation.

While student affairs practitioners are typically responsible for learning and student development that occurs outside of the classroom (American College Personnel Association, 1994), many practitioners also teach in college and university classrooms. Student affairs professionals instruct a variety of courses, from first-year success seminars to functional area specific courses to leadership classes (Moore & Marsh, 2007). Higher education research has not fully explored the experiences of these student affairs professionals who teach formal, credit-bearing classes. Furthermore, the experiences of these professionals who hold marginalized identities, such as women of color, are almost absent from the literature. This chapter aims to illuminate the experiences of new and entry-level women of color student affairs practitioners who have taught and continue to teach in predominantly and historically White college classrooms.

OUR FRAMEWORK

Narratives and storytelling can serve an extremely powerful role in marginalized communities, particularly in supporting healing and liberation (Solórzano & Yosso, 2002). We share our own narratives and those of our participants throughout the chapter, specifically focusing on the challenges we faced and strategies we utilized to overcome hurdles, be effective educators, and thrive in our work. We do so using the framework of critical race feminism and the knowledge gained from conducting a qualitative research study on the topic of women of color student affairs professionals who teach in predominantly and historically White college classrooms.

Critical Race Feminism

The framework for this chapter is critical race feminism (CRF), which is a critical theory that aims to understand the intersections of race and gender in relation to power (Wing, 1997). CRF originates from critical race theory (CRT; Ladson-Billings & Tate, 2006; Solórzano & Yosso, 2002). Legal scholars developed CRT to provide critical analysis of the intersections of law, race, and racism. A central tenet of CRF is the importance of counter-narratives, specifically uplifting the narratives of women of color that are often pushed to the margins (Moraga & Anzaldúa, 2001). There are two key concepts of CRF that we utilize in this chapter: intersectionality and anti-essentialism (Grillo, 1995). Together, these concepts illustrate that every woman comprises a complex web of identities, such as their race, class, age, and gender identities. Thus, no woman's experience can be understood without acknowledging all her intersecting identities (Grillo, 1995). We utilize CRF as a framework for sharing the unique experiences of women of color student affairs practitioners when they teach in White college classrooms.

Our Study

This chapter is a counter-story to the dominant narratives that suggest women of color student affairs professionals do not belong as instructors in college classrooms. We present our counter-story by sharing our own experiences and those of participants in a collaborative autoethnographic study we conducted. Collaborative autoethnography (CAE) is a qualitative research method where researchers make meaning of autobiographical data to gain sociocultural understandings of their experiences (Anderson, 2010; Chang, 2008; Ellis, 2004; Reed-Danahay, 1997). CAE allows individuals with a shared experience to collectively relay and make meaning of the sociocultural phenomena demonstrated in their experiences (Chang, Ngunjiri, & Hernandez, 2012), participating in counter-storytelling as they do so. In our study, six participants, including ourselves, engaged in individual data collection surrounding their teaching experiences. In each collaborative session, participants shared their individual data and reflections, engaged in storytelling, and processed their experiences with others.

LESSONS LEARNED

Preparing for the Challenges

While we face numerous challenges as women of color professionals, the added dynamics of teaching in predominantly White classrooms exacerbate the difficulties we experience. As new and entry-level practitioners, we learned the importance of acknowledging, accepting, and preparing for the issues that may emerge for us to be effective educators.

Students make assumptions about our abilities based on how we appear in the classroom, namely based on our race, gender, and age. We have realized these assumptions often take the shape and form of questions to our authority (Ng, 1997; Vargas, 2002). I, Nadeeka, experienced this directly when I taught an undergraduate leadership course during my student affairs master's program. As I was debriefing my classroom experience with other instructors of different sections who were members of my master's cohort, I realized there was a drastic difference in how students were addressing my White counterparts in comparison to how they addressed my woman of color co-instructor and me. Students were calling a White male instructor "professor" in class and addressing him as "doctor" in emails. These occurrences contrasted greatly to my experience in the classroom where my co-instructor and I were questioned directly about our ability to be instructors and were never assumed to have doctorate degrees. These events led me to understand the importance of naming my degrees and level of experience when I introduce myself to new classrooms of students. While this sometimes feels in conflict with my values of critical pedagogy (Freire, 2000) where power and knowledge are shared among students and instructors, I recognize I still work within institutions that require me, as an instructor, to determine grades and maintain a level of control over my classroom. Other participants in our study had similar experiences of discrepancy in titles given to them compared to their White counterparts. One participant shared that she was initially more distant and formal with her students to create a sense of authority. We wrestled with the conflict of needing or desiring "authority" in the classroom as many of us also strived to use anti-oppressive pedagogies (Freire, 2000). These stories illustrate that establishing authority as a classroom instructor is tricky but important. We must demonstrate to students that we have the ability and competence to be their instructors, while also working to create a learning environment where knowledge is shared among students and instructors. Individuals who oversee the instructional process and coordinate course sections may also play a role in helping women of color instructors establish respect in the classroom. They can support instructors by helping them navigate the first few classes and can communicate instructors' roles to students in an effective way that helps to legitimize them.

Some of the biggest challenges faced by women of color arise when integrating social justice concepts into our curriculum. For our participants and us, social justice and equity are core values and motivation for our work in higher education. Thus, we felt it was imperative to integrate issues of privilege, power, and oppression into our curriculum in our various teaching roles. However, we were often faced with resistance by students with dominant identities, typically because they saw us, with our marginalized identities, as promoting our "own agendas." To respond to this phenomenon, we prepared extensively, unlike our counterparts, by brainstorming questions in advance, strategically introducing issues of privilege and oppression, and inviting colleagues with dominant identities to facilitate social justice dialogues.

I, Ginny, taught a course early in my career as a student affairs professional at a predominantly White institution. As I reflect on that experience, I remember the precaution I took to ensure I did not make any mistakes in the classroom. When I was preparing for class and writing my lessons, I felt like I could not have any errors because students would notice them and make assumptions about my intelligence, ability, or right to be in the classroom space as an instructor.

I, Nadeeka, shared Ginny's experience during my first teaching experience in graduate school. My co-facilitator and I would spend long afternoons planning our lessons for the week, meticulously choosing specific questions with certain language we felt would be the least intimidating. We felt we had to do this diligent planning to introduce certain social justice concepts and have a productive discussion with our class of predominantly White students. We had a shared online folder of resources and course materials with another set of instructors, who were both White. As we looked through their materials we realized that they did not necessarily do as intensive of lesson planning as us, especially on lessons exploring identity and power. As I have taught more classes as a new and entry-level professional, I have found the privileged identity exploration model (Watt, 2007) to be a useful tool for understanding and more effectively responding to defensive reactions of students.

When facilitating social justice lessons in the classroom, we also struggled with the tension of balancing the education of students with dominant identities and the support of marginalized students. I, Aliya, struggled with teaching lessons on issues of social justice during my first teaching experience as a new professional because of the need to challenge dominant ideology while supporting marginalized students. I would wonder, "How do I respond to this White student who just said something problematic without causing him to disengage, but while also trying to not further harm the student of color that is sitting next to him in the classroom?" This tension was shared by other participants regarding the need to balance the education of students with dominant identities on issues of privilege with the desire to prevent further oppression of students with marginalized identities. One of our participants shared the frustration she felt in this balancing act:

> It makes me really angry sometimes because I think that, particularly as women of color, we think about these things in ways that our colleagues, particularly our White male colleagues, do not. They will let dominant ideologies just dominate the classroom and expect students with marginalized identities to just get on board or get over it. But we will sit here and agonize over how we can find a way where everybody is happy, everybody feels heard, and everybody is affirmed.

As we grow and learn as student affairs professionals and instructors, we will continue to develop strategies to address problematic comments and to lessen the likelihood that those with dominant identities will disengage when they experience cognitive dissonance (Watt, 2007). Understanding that we will face challenges and setbacks, especially during our first few teaching experiences as new and entry-level professionals, was helpful in facilitating resilience and increased motivation. Reflection on our own teaching tactics and experiences, along with reading articles and books about pedagogy and instructional methods, can support our growth as educators. Supervisors can encourage and provide space for this learning and exploration through asking reflective questions during meetings and allowing time for women of color practitioners to learn new strategies. It is important to understand that learning how to be an effective social justice educator and raising the critical consciousness of students is a lifelong journey and process.

Engaging in Reflection

The process of sharing narratives offered us a sense of validation because it allowed for us to engage in critical reflection, self-reflection, and processing of our thoughts about our teaching experiences. Critical reflection serves two purposes: (a) It helps the educator understand how power supports and frames many educational processes, and (b) It supports the educator in questioning hegemonic assumptions and practices in teaching (Brookfield, 1995). Reflection also impacts the knowledge, skills, and character of an educator (Shandomo, 2010). The process of individually reflecting and journaling and then sharing our thoughts in group dialogue provided us with knowledge to serve as better practitioners and instructors.

One reflection tool is writing, which gives the opportunity for one to re-member, recreate, and reconstruct what is learned and can be learned from a teaching experience (Shandomo, 2010). Journaling can take place formal-ly and informally through prompts, scheduled logging, or whenever needed to process an experience. We recommend journaling because it follows our approach of making meaning of our experiences. By maintaining a reflec-tive practice, new and entry-level women of color who teach in White college classrooms can see how their teaching practices, interactions with students, and educator identities have changed or improved.

Sharing our experiences with one another was just as important as per-sonal reflection. Women of color practitioners can reach out to mentors and colleagues to discuss their experiences in the classroom. Supervisors and individuals coordinating the instructional process can help create space for reflection for women of color practitioners. For new and entry-level professionals, having the ability and space to share stories can be a liberating and encouraging experience.

Advocating for Ourselves

As women of color working at predominantly White institutions, we of-ten feel obligated to take on additional responsibilities, especially those that support marginalized students. Teaching courses may be one of those additional tasks, which may then result in further undertakings such as writ-ing letters of recommendation, mentoring individual students of color, and advising student of color organizations. There is a tension in feeling the burden of these additional responsibilities and a simultaneous desire to un-dertake them for the benefit of students. We comprehend the importance of our representation for students of color and the value we bring to class-rooms; however, we also understand the feeling of being tokenized and un-derappreciated. One participant in our study shared that she was asked to teach a particular class *because* of her identity as a woman of color—she felt the coordinators of the class desired a token minority to teach the course. However, she also recognized that her presence in the classroom was im-portant as positive representation for students of color.

While we may feel compelled to perform this extra labor because of our own values, we can still ask for recognition and compensation. We must learn how to advocate for ourselves, especially when our time, emotional energy, and physical labor are utilized. We need to hold institutions ac-countable for operationalizing political, educational, and social power structures that affect our ability to teach. We can do this by addressing challenges through difficult dialogues and naming our experiences (Rodriguez, Boahene, Gonzales-Howell, & Anesi, 2012). Sharing our lived experiences frees us from being silenced or dismissed by our students, colleagues, and university administrators (Rodriguez et al., 2012).

Self-advocacy can be challenging, especially when we may doubt our abilities as instructors. As women of color, we often experience imposter syndrome, which are feelings of phoniness and self-doubt, and an inability to take credit for our accomplishments (Brems, Baldwin, Davis, & Namyniuk, 1994). The added role of instructor can often result in further feelings of imposter syndrome. While we may feel like imposters in the classroom at times, we must recognize the unique strengths and talents we bring. As one participant in our study elaborated, "We don't have to have permission to own our positions, own our authority, own our particular voice."

Finally, practicing self-care is vital to sustaining ourselves as educators and practitioners (Burke, Dye, & Hughey, 2016). Self-care also requires advocacy, through advocating to our supervisors and to ourselves, to make time for our own renewal and wellness. Our bodies, minds, and spirits feel the stress and impact of racism and other forms of oppression. As women of color, taking care of ourselves is a form of resistance of the status quo (Lorde, 1988). To continue with our social justice education within and outside of the classroom, we must prioritize our own self-care and wellness.

Finding Support From Our Institution

Women of color student affairs professionals who teach in predominantly White classrooms are engaging in a challenging task. Each time we enter the classroom, we bring our time and efforts of lesson planning, our identities, and our lived experiences. We may experience stereotype threat, imposter syndrome, microaggressions, invalidations, questions to our authority, and discomfort from our experiences in the classroom.

Recognizing the unique benefits that student affairs practitioners bring to the classroom, institutions should offer formal and informal opportunities for women of color practitioners to learn pedagogical techniques and classroom management strategies. Universities could open the existing support systems for faculty, like seminars and instructional support departments, and allow student affairs professionals to receive these forms of assistance. In our collaborative sessions, participants shared the desire to have access to the seminars and training opportunities that exist for improving the teaching methods of faculty members. One of our participants described that, as student affairs professionals,

> We don't have access to some of these faculty resources to continue our pro-
> fessional development, especially around curriculum development and class-
> room management. When we actually have access, it doesn't mean I have the
> time to utilize it, so that is the other barrier there.

This narrative speaks to the importance of providing compensation or a reduction of workload when practitioners take on an instructional role, in addition to offering the trainings and resources to which faculty have access.

Administrators and supervisors can support women of color student affairs professionals who take on teaching responsibilities by offering some
sort of compensation. This can range from actual monetary compensation
for their additional labor or a reduction in workload from their current
work responsibilities. Women of color student affairs professionals typically
receive little or no compensation for their roles as instructors. In our study,
of the six participants who taught a variety of courses over their years as
practitioners, only two had received course credit during their graduate
studies for their teaching responsibilities (Boss et al., 2019). We did not
receive any additional compensation for every other instructor role we un-
dertook as student affairs practitioners. The additional responsibilities out-
lined previously make the lack of compensation particularly troublesome to
equity and labor practices.

Establishing Networking and Professional Development

We advocate for providing mentorship and professional development
for women of color student affairs professionals. Mentors for entry-level
women of color professionals provide the mentee with feedback and guidance at the beginning of their teaching careers (Rodriguez et al., 2012). Establishing mentor networks, formal or informal, has been a recommended
practice for supporting women of color pursuing faculty roles (Dancy II &
Brown II, 2011; Smith, 2016). Institutions can support women of color student affairs professionals who teach by facilitating opportunities for these
women to meet for professional and social gatherings.

Professional development opportunities (e.g., national and local conferences, networking events, open forums, collaborative research, seminars,
etc.) allow women of color student affairs practitioners to connect with other professionals, especially if there is a limited number of mentors at their
respective institutions. As a graduate student, I, Carol, co-facilitated conference sessions on women of color who teach in predominantly White classrooms with the other authors of this chapter. I was nervous about the sessions
because I feared that no one would show up or be interested in the topic.

However, the sessions filled with women of color student affairs professionals who needed the space to process their teaching experiences. We told stories about our challenges and successes and had the opportunity to network and exchange contact information. These were uplifting moments for me as an entry-level professional, as I found myself feeling less isolated, knowing that there is a community of women who are here to support each other.

Mentorship networks for women of color can also be formed via online communities. Steele and Korn (2016) suggest that social media mentoring for women of color in academia can serve to break down barriers of traditional mentorship and encourage the development of multiple mentors, the holistic self, and peer-mentoring. Mentorship cannot be understated as a tool for empowering and retaining women of color who teach in predominantly White classrooms. We utilized social media networks to find our participants and engaged in further mentoring opportunities. When I was a graduate student, I, Carol, could use Facebook groups to gain access to opportunities and resources and embrace feelings of validation as a woman of color student affairs professional in the classroom. Online communities of scholar-practitioners inspired my work and kept me motivated to pursue my journey as an educator. Because of these spaces, I felt that my experiences were validated and I had the support of professional networks and organizations.

We Are Not Alone

As women of color student affairs professionals who have taught in White college classrooms, we bring our stories and truths to light to support new and entry-level professionals embarking on their journey as educators. We hope the experiences we have shared can illuminate our realities in the classroom and provide a sense of connection to other women of color professionals. You are not alone. We hope by writing this chapter, we provide some space for you to feel safer and braver in writing, speaking, and sharing your narratives. We hope to support your healing process; thereby, we can uplift this community and support each other in our growth and development as women of color student affairs professionals who teach in White college classrooms.

REFERENCES

American College Personnel Association. (1994). *The student learning imperative: Implications for student affairs.* Retrieved from http://www.myacpa.org/files/acpas-student-learning-imperativepdf

Anderson, K. J. (2010). Students' stereotypes of professors: An exploration of the double violations of ethnicity and gender. *Social Psychology of Education, 13*(4), 459–472. https://doi.org/10.1007/s11218-010-9121-3

Boss, G. J., Karunaratne, N., Huang, C., Beavers, A., Pegram-Floyd, V., & Tullos, K.C. (2019). It's a double-edged sword": A collaborative autoethnography of women of color higher education and student affairs administrators who teach in the college classroom. *Journal of Women and Gender in Higher Education.*

Brems, C., Baldwin, M. R., Davis, L., & Namyniuk, L. (1994). The imposter syndrome as related to teaching evaluations and advising relationships of university faculty members. *The Journal of Higher Education, 65*(2), 183–193. https://doi.org/10.2307/2943923

Brookfield, S. (1995). *Becoming a critically reflective teacher.* San Francisco, CA: Jossey-Bass.

Burke, M. G., Dye, L., & Hughey, A. W. (2016). Teaching mindfulness for the self-care and well-being of student affairs professionals. *College Student Affairs Journal, 34*(3), 93–107. https://doi.org/10.1353/csj.2016.0021

Chang, H. (2008). *Autoethnography as method.* Walnut Creek, CA: Left Coast Press.

Chang, H., Ngunjiri, F., & Hernandez, K. C. (2012). *Collaborative autoethnography.* Walnut Creek, CA: Left Coast Press.

Dancy II, T., & Brown II, M. (2011). The mentoring and induction of educators of color: Addressing the impostor syndrome in academe. *Journal of School Leadership, 21*(4) 607–634.

Ellis, C. (2004). *The ethnographic I: A methodological novel about autoethnography.* Walnut Creek, CA: AltaMira Press.

Freire, P. (2000). *Pedagogy of the oppressed* (30th anniversary ed.). New York, NY: Continuum.

Grillo, T. (1995). Anti-essentialism and intersectionality: Tools to dismantle the master's house. *Berkeley Women's Law Journal, 10*(1), 16–30.

Ladson-Billings, G., & Tate, W. (2006). Toward a critical race theory of education. In A. Dixson & C. Rousseau (Eds.), *Critical race theory in education* (pp. 11–30). New York, NY: Routledge.

Lorde, A. (1988). *A burst of light: Essays.* Ithaca, NY: Firebrand Books.

Moore, E. L., & Marsh, R. S. (2007). College teaching for student affairs professionals. In E. L. Moore (Ed.), Special issue: Student affairs staff as teachers (pp. 3–11). *New Directions for Student Services,* No. 117. San Francisco, CA: Jossey-Bass.

Moraga, C., & Anzaldúa, G. (2001). *This bridge called my back: Writings by radical women of color.* Berkeley, CA: Third Woman.

Ng, R. (1997). A woman out of control: Deconstructing sexism and racism in the university. In J. Glazer-Raymo, B. Townsend, & B. Ropers-Huliman (Eds.), *Women in higher education: A feminist perspective* (pp. 360–370). Boston, MA: Pearson Custom.

Reed-Danahay, D. (1997). *Auto/ethnography: Rewriting the self and the social.* Oxford: Berg.

Rodriguez, D., Boahene, A. O., Gonzalez-Howell, N., & Anesi, J. (2012). Practicing liberatory pedagogy. *Cultural Studies ↔ Critical Methodologies, 12*(2), 96–108. https://doi.org/10.1177/1532708611435211

Shandomo, H. M. (2010). The role of critical reflection in teacher education. *School–University Partnerships, 4*(1), 101–113.

Smith, M. (2016). Walking the tightrope of academe with no net. In B. L. H. Marina & S. Ross (Eds.), *Beyond Retention: Cultivating spaces of equity, justice, and fairness for women of color in U.S. higher education* (pp. 25–45). Charlotte, NC: Information Age.

Solórzano, D., & Yosso, T. (2002). Critical race methodology: Counter-storytelling as an analytical framework for education research. *Qualitative Inquiry, 8,* 23–44. https://doi.org/10.1177/107780040200800103

Steele, C. K., & Korn, J. U. (2016). Mentors and sister friends: The intersections of race, multiplicity, and holism with online social media. In K. Tassie & S. Givens (Eds.), *Women of color navigating mentoring relationships: Critical examinations* (pp. 165–178). Lanham, MD: Lexington Books.

Vargas, L. (2002). *Women faculty of color in the White classroom: Narratives on the pedagogical implications of teacher education.* New York, NY: Peter Lang.

Watt, S. K. (2007). Difficult dialogues, privilege, and social justice: Uses of the privileged identity exploration (PIE) model in student affairs practice. *The College Student Affairs Journal, 26*(2), 114–126.

Wing, A. K. (Ed.). (1997). *Critical race feminism: A reader.* New York, NY: New York University Press.

CHAPTER 10

WHEN GRATEFUL ISN'T GOOD ENOUGH

How African-American Women Can Successfully and Strategically Navigate Professionally in Student Affairs

Jasmine M. Kelly
Georgia State University

Drawing upon entry-level professional experiences as a framework, this chapter will illustrate why it is imperative that African-American women find their voice and lean in to themselves workwise despite microaggressions, stereotypes, misconceptions, bullying, generational stereotypes, and other foreseen and unforeseen barriers. It is acceptable for them to make change and choices as they see fit. This chapter will draw upon the Womanism social theory to frame why African-American women speaking up in the workplace is considered a political act. This chapter is especially appropriate for women of color in student affairs who are working in hostile work environments, seeking professional growth, and trying to find their place in higher education.

No Ways Tired, pages 87–93
Copyright © 2019 by Information Age Publishing
All rights of reproduction in any form reserved.

Black women have been and still are integral to the well-being of their fami-lies, their communities, and the nation through their work, entrepreneur-ship, caregiving, political participation, and more. They create opportuni-ties for themselves and their loved ones while improving our economy and society. Although they have all the makings to be a success, their contri-butions are often undervalued and undercompensated. Whether one ex-amines Black women's access to healthcare, earnings, or access to much needed social supports like childcare and eldercare, Black women are get-ting the short end of the stick despite having contributed so much to the building on this nation (National Domestic Workers Alliance, 2016).

It is no secret that wherever Black women find themselves, they must cre-ate a safe-space to sustain and thrive. There are not many African-American women in leadership and power positions and the unwritten rule is, *once you get there, stay there.* Despite an increasing presence in student affairs, Black female administrators continue to face barriers that limit their advance-ment from mid-level to senior-level positions (Belk, 2006). Due to the dual-ity of race and gender, there is a unique challenge for Black women to gain access to career networks which is critical for advancement to upper level administrative and leadership positions (Burke & Carter, 2015). Honestly, as a Black woman who is new to the profession, this context scares me. It is frightening because I fear that all my professional development will be in vain due to this glass ceiling.

LESSONS LEARNED EARLY

Essentially, I grew up in a single-parent household. Even though my mother and father were married, it became very clear quite early that my mom was the primary breadwinner. It resonated with me that despite having a man in the house, it is ultimately up to me to make sure that I am okay. A man being present in a household does not always equate to emotional, mental, and in my mother's case, financial security. My mother did not finish col-lege and throughout my childhood and currently, I have watched her work very hard; more than I wish she had to at times. Witnessing my mother's hard work, I always told myself that I did not want to be in the same posi-tion if I could help it. Therefore, I decided to graduate from college, have a career, and of course when the time came, have a significant other present who could ultimately contribute to my big picture. While I have not crossed paths with someone worthy enough to be a part of the "big picture," I can proudly say that I have obtained two degrees, am working in my career field, and have enough money for Forever 21 once I pay bills. Obviously, life is golden and there is no need to rock the boat—or so I thought.

Growing up observing my mother greatly formed my professional work ethic. I have always made it a point to work hard, have a purpose to everything that I do and more so, to not be afraid to move when a situation is no longer healthy for me. Understanding that situations can shift without notice, I always understood that I had to invest in myself. Thus, when I was applying for jobs before I finished graduate school, I sought positions where I could grow and where I could make an impact.

MY FIRST JOB

Although I left Atlanta, Georgia, to attend college in Kentucky, as luck would have it, my first professional position would land me back in my hometown of Atlanta. After two interviews and a salary that I could live with, I gladly accepted a position as an academic advisor for first-year students at a local community college in June 2016. I was ecstatic about the position as I would be working with at-risk students and I had the chance to work around "my people" again. In contrast to my educational and professional experience at my graduate institution, I found myself in a work environment where 90% of the population looked like me. Educationally and professionally, I knew that representation was important to me. Furthermore, I was very satisfied in my role as an academic advisor and I enjoyed the work I was doing. As I adjusted to my role as a new professional, I became confident in my abilities. I loved working with my advising colleagues and I appreciated having a very supportive director. For the first time in a long time in my life, I believed things were going well and began to establish a new normal.

I began to feel the need to change my position a few months later after my institution entered what my director deemed as an "enrollment crisis." My institution's attendance numbers were low and more than half of the student population had not yet registered for their spring semester classes. Call it naivety, but I was not the least bit worried because I was confident in my abilities as an academic advisor and under the guidance of my director; I knew a plan would be devised soon. Yes, I understood that low enrollment means less money, which had the possibility to threaten my job, but I remained optimistic. In efforts to dig the institution out of the enrollment hole, the academic advising department, in essence, began to only advise at-risk students and under the guise of the enrollment crisis, my department took on the responsibility of ensuring that all students were registered for the spring semester. What accompanied this initiative were longer work days, shortened lunch breaks, and overworked advisors. Yet and still, I thought such outcomes came with the first-year of employment for student affairs professionals. Therefore, I decided to just grin and bear it while cultivating my work ethic.

It was not until December of 2016, during an institutional meeting led by the president, that I was sure my position an academic advisor at that college was no longer conducive to my professional growth. In short, the institution's president reprimanded a faculty member in front of campus members and visiting stakeholders for minutes on end. Witnessing my campus leader behaving in such a way really disturbed me and I concluded that if the college president can talk so nastily to a faculty member, then how could they possibly care about my growth and development as a new professional. There were other factors that weighed into my thoughts about leaving the position such as even though I was not in a leadership position, I was working a "decent" job that I went to school for and I had money left to spend after all my bills were paid. Furthermore, in the eyes of my family, my mother specifically, I made it. Thus, one could only imagine the pressure I felt when I decided to leave my first position in student affairs.

Without a doubt, leadership sets the tone for professional growth. A major aspect of creating an institutional climate is trust and advocacy. According to Ruthkosky (2013), trust is a reciprocal phenomenon in respect to relationships between senior student affairs officers and their subordinates. To maintain a genuine trust in their leaders, subordinates need to believe that they are being trusted in return. When the president chewed out my colleague, I knew that all my trust in him was gone. If he could reprimand someone so harshly in front of campus visitors, I knew there was no hope for me. Additionally, if he could do such a thing to an employee without first questioning her train of thought, such behavior shows that he had no faith in his subordinates. It was definitely time to go.

TO MOVE OR NOT TO MOVE

Womanist 1. From *womanish*. (Opp. of "girlish," i.e., frivolous, irresponsible, not serious). A Black feminist or feminist of color. From the Black folk expression of mothers to female children, "You acting womanish," that is, like a woman. Usually referring to outrageous, audacious, courageous, or *willful* behavior. Wanting to know more and in greater depth than is considered "good" for one. Interested in grown-up doings. Acting grown up. Being grown up. Interchangeable with another Black folk expression: "You trying to be grown." Responsible. In charge. *Serious*. ("Womanist by Alice Walker," n.d.)

When I went home that day, I told my mother about my day and my decision to look for new employment. During our conversation, I made sure to not just complain about what occurred that day but to offer substantial reasoning for my decision. Although my mother understood my plight, her response was the one I expected to receive—stay at the job for the simple sake of having a job. I understood the place from which her wisdom derived as my mother cared for my well-being and in her eyes, the threat of lack of professional growth and development was not a major issue. My mother reminded me that I worked so hard to get to where I am and that I should not let something "as small as what the president did" (her words) hinder me. Essentially, job security was the main focus. I took heed to her advice and I thought that my mind would change, but days later, I felt the same way and began to search for a new position.

While I continued my search for a new position, I could not help but to become annoyed at the responses I received from friends and loved ones about my decision to search for a new job. I understood they were coming from a loving place, but I could not understand why they would want me to remain in an environment that was not at all conducive to my growth and development. In essence, I felt that the underlying message I received from each person I talked to about my situation was that I was "doing too much" for someone in my position. True, I was a new student affairs professional but in my eyes, being new gave me more reason to be aware about everything that was occurring around me.

Feeling like I began to give in to what everyone else was saying about my situation, I reached out to my mentors who have been employed in higher education longer. I called those who I met at conferences prior and I even consulted my former professor. My mentors and former professor understood how I felt nonetheless, told me that no situation is perfect and that the choice was ultimately up to me. They made me feel so much better because they served as a sounding board for me and even though it was not their situation now, they validated how I felt. Some of my mentors even told me about some of the crazy circumstances they had to encounter. Amid all the madness, I was so thankful to have a community of Black women to call upon. I was more than grateful and having that community helped me to cope with my situation better because I knew I was not the only one.

I instantly began to think of the womanism social theory when processing how some of my friends and family members perceived me in relation to my situation. Yes, they were listening to how I felt, but in a sense, I knew they thought *who is she to feel this way? She is just getting started!* In short, my wanting to navigate so quickly from what was perceived as an already good job was too much for me. Moreover, I know that if I felt this way during my circumstances, I also knew that countless other Black women felt the same way and were also probably being told that they were "doing too much." Saying such things to Black women can be very detrimental because we may doubt our own feelings and beliefs and stay in toxic environments just so we won't be perceived negatively, which is dangerous.

It was during my moments of confusion that I chose to create some clarity and decided I was not going to give into the status quo. I knew that it was up to me to position myself to grow and thrive professionally. Besides, if I did not do it, who else would? Furthermore, I should not be deemed as being professionally irresponsible because I was willing to reposition myself at such an early time in my career. Thus, I decided that I was going to continue to always work hard, put my best foot forward at my job, and do the same in a new position. At the same time, I was not going to allow myself to stay in professional positions that were no longer conducive to my growth. I confidently began to search for a new job and I felt more validated than ever.

SURVIVAL

*Caring for myself is not self-indulgence, it is self-preservation,
and that is an act of political warfare.*

—Lorde, 2017

Black women's existence itself is a political act. We are always caring for, loving, and protecting others. However, when that same energy is turned inward it becomes a problem. It becomes an issue when we no longer take whatever is thrown toward us, when we begin to speak up for ourselves, and when we begin to have preferences. Our existence is radical because simply being ourselves is an act of protest. If we are at the disposal of others, we are okay, but the minute we speak up, we become the "loudmouth," the "sassy one," or "ungrateful." For that reason, Black women should not possess any doubt when it comes to making decisions that create an atmosphere of peace, serenity, safety, and happiness for themselves. Unfortunately, from personal experience, I know this is easier said than done and the doing is much more difficult. If an African American woman who is a new professional finds herself in a position that is like my own, I strongly urge them to lean into themselves and make the necessary changes. There is no shame at all in survival and even more, no explanation is needed.

REFERENCES

Belk, A. (2006). *Perceptions of career advancement factors held by Black student affairs administrators: A gender comparison* (Doctoral dissertation). Florida State University. Retrieved from https://pdfs.semanticscholar.org/9e7d/94656e201f5 8f0fc8ff20726da2793738503.pdf

Burke, M. G., & Carter, J. D. (2015). Examining perceptions of networking among African American women in student affairs. *NASPA Journal About Women in Higher Education, 8*(2), 140–155. https://doi.org/10.1080/19407882.2015 .1057165

Lorde, A. (2017). GoodReads. *Quotable quote. P.1.* Retrieved from https://www
.goodreads.com/quotes/437563-caring-for-myself-is-not-self-indulgence-it
-is-self-preservation-and

National Domestic Workers Alliance. (2016). *The status of Black women in the United
States.* Retrieved from https://www.domesticworkers.org/status-black-women
-united-states

Ruthkosky, P. J. (2013). A multiperspective analysis on developing and maintaining
trust in senior student affairs leadership. *Journal of Student Affairs Research and
Practice, 50*(2), 171–188. https://doi.org/10.1515/jsarp-2013-0013

Womanist by Alice Walker. (n.d.). Retrieved from http://womanistwork.com/

CHAPTER 11

RESILIENCY IN UPSTATE NEW YORK

Three Young Professionals of Color and Their Journeys to Support Each Other

Vigor W. H. Lam
Cornell University

Catherine M. Ramirez
Cornell University

Marcus E. Scales
Cornell University

Renn and Hodges (2007) noted in the NASPA Journal that despite the availability of research about graduate preparation of new professionals, it has been more than 25 years since the publication of an open-ended study of the experience of new professionals. There is an even larger gap in literature for professionals of color. This chapter highlights three student affairs practitioners living in Upstate New York, working with students of color, recounting their experiences as young professionals of color.

No Ways Tired, pages 95–104
Copyright © 2019 by Information Age Publishing
All rights of reproduction in any form reserved.

As professionals of color who are new to the field, we wished there had been literature that discussed best practices and how to stay resilient in the field, especially at a predominantly White institution (PWI). While we represent the voices of professionals of Asian American, Latina/o/x, and Black racial identities, we are only a few voices of many in the field. We hope to create space and dialogue surrounding retention of new professionals of color and common issues they may face working as they transition to their first and/or second professional role post- masters.

LITERATURE REVIEW

The field of student affairs can be as rewarding as it is exhausting. The altruistic undertones in our field encourage professionals to go above and beyond as a minimum standard of work. According to Marshall, Gardener, Hughes, and Lowery (2016), student affairs professionals leave the field for multiple reasons including burnout, lack of supervisory support, and ability to fit in the institutional culture. At least half of new professionals that enter the field leave within 5 years (Tull, 2006). However, there is a limited amount of research available specifically on practitioners of color. We have identified two topics that are pertinent to our experiences in our review of literature—self-authorship and "two- to three-year experiences."

Self-Authorship

Robert Kegan (1994) articulated the developmental concept of self-authorship as a necessary foundation for adults to meet typical expectations they face at work, home, and school; such as the ability to be self-initiating, guided by their own visions, responsible for their experience, and able to develop interdependent relations with diverse others. Baxter Magolda, as cited in Evans, Forney, Guido, Patton, and Renn (2010), highlighted several developmental tasks associated with the decade of the twenties, including values exploration, making sense of information gained about the world in previous years, determining the path one will take and taking steps along that path. Self-authorship can be used by adults who experience oppression as the ability to deconstruct racist messages (an epistemological capacity) is crucial to denouncing those messages to create a positive racial or ethnic identity that in turn supports authentic relations with diverse others (Torres & Baxter Magolda, 2004; Torres & Hernandez, 2007). As new professionals in the field, we encountered these messages covertly and overtly at our workplaces and in our town.

Two- to Three-Year Experiences

Effective supervision of new professionals is one way that the profession can reduce the propensity of new professionals to leave (Tull, 2006). Supervision in higher education, as defined by Winston and Creamer (1997) is "a management function intended to promote the achievement of institutional goals and enhance the personal and professional capabilities of staff. Supervision interprets the institutional mission and focuses human and fiscal resources on the promotion of individual and organizational competence" (p. 42).

Janosik and Creamer (2003) wrote, "Supervision of people always is important to an organization and is a key ingredient in any staffing plan, but supervision of new professionals may be among the most critical supervision tasks or responsibilities of a college or university" (p. 1). When supervising employees, Winston and Creamer (1998) noted that supervisors should establish an open, trusting relationship with the employee; determine their career anchor; identify their professional aspirations; and identify necessary knowledge and skills for them to advance professionally. An effective model of supervision that provides the necessary orientation and socialization to student affairs and higher education is one way to reduce the attrition of new professionals.

Self-authorship and "two- to three-year experiences" are topics that are important for us to highlight, as we discuss our stories in getting into the field. Our personal narratives that follow, center on our family histories, our personal identities, and our journeys into student affairs.

PERSONAL NARRATIVES

Vigor Wei Hon Lam

As a first-generation college student, gay, and Chinese American, I have always appreciated my roots and how my parents immigrated to the United States. They have sacrificed so much for me—moving to a predominantly White, upper middle-class neighborhood with immense educational resources and helping support my path to higher education.

At my undergraduate alma mater, The Ohio State University, my experience as a very involved student leader in the Asian American community gave me exposure to administrators and staff within the multicultural center as the president of Asian American Association, a member of Pi Delta Psi Fraternity, Incorporated, and the leadership team of Midwest Asian American Students Union (MAASU). In getting to know my student organization advisors and the staff, I was encouraged to apply and pursue a career in higher education and student affairs. As a landscape architecture and design student at the time, I did not have time or energy to be a resident assistant or orientation leader, as many in those roles typically enter the field on a traditional path. Many of my hours were spent in the studio working on design projects. One of the main reasons I have come to understand my being in the field of higher education is the ability to work and support the intersectional identities of students, especially those that share mine of being gay and Asian. As an undergraduate student, I did not have an advisor who I could truly say shared very similar struggles that I did in understanding my identities.

As I have worked in the field for the past 3 years post-masters, I have been in two professional roles in academic affairs and multicultural affairs, both at PWIs and elite institutions. In both roles, I have been managed by mid-level professionals who have not supervised professional, full-time staff, until my role. This circumstance caused me to have dissonance in how to convey the growth and ambition I have and how to thrive in campus culture and navigate politics. As every campus has its own political culture and nuances that are unspoken, I experienced much of this in my professional roles. At very large and elite institutions, a hierarchy is engrained in the organizational culture. I was actively discouraged from reaching out to those from which I sought mentorship who were multiple chains above me in management and/or in another division. This impediment was exceptionally difficult for me as I was seeking ways to find mentorship and support from professionals of color at an institution and city that is predominantly White.

I have considered leaving the field already on several occasions. In Chinese culture, filial piety is commonplace and I have found myself with internal conflict—being in a field that is affirming to my identities but doesn't provide enough paid labor to support the village that brought me into the profession. Professionals who enter the field typically enter by way of their student involvement and/or job(s) on campus and their degree major is usually not related to education. Having not pursued a career in architecture post-graduation, I have considered going back to school to pursue a master's degree in architecture and/or a PhD in a related field. As I reflect on the field of higher education and my professional ambitions, I have come to understand that university administration as a career will not be my entire career. Some of these other ambitions include having a joint appointment or consulting career in both higher education administration and architecture/design. I have since left the field after being recruited by a construction management firm to work on the program management team on a multi-year master plan for a community college, combining my passions in architecture, construction, and education.

Catherine M. Ramírez

Being a student affairs practitioner was not on my list of prospective careers. As a first-generation college student whose parents immigrated from

Colombia, I did not have the knowledge about the possibilities of careers within higher education. I started my college career at a community college and later transferred to a large public institution. It was not until I transferred, that I was able to get involved in student organizations and start to realize that I could work in a higher education setting. When I served as an undergraduate program coordinator, I learned about the variety of tasks and different functional areas in which I could work. I appreciated the flexibility that the field offered and was determined to help future students like me succeed at any institution.

As a graduate student, I had the opportunity of working at the most racially diverse institution in the nation and at a Hispanic serving instituion (HSI) during a summer internship. These experiences cemented my focus and dedication to advocating and removing barriers for students from historically underrepresented identities within higher education. My work environment, supervisors, and colleagues helped to create a sense of belonging where I thrived. Additionally, seeing professionals who shared similar identities and experiences as me in supervisory roles and senior leadership positions at the institution validated my aspirations to achieve highly in the field. I knew that my family made several sacrifices for me to be able to have the opportunities to pursue higher education and I was not about to let all their hard work be in vain.

After graduating, I took a position at an institution in upstate New York. Coming from a vastly diverse institution located in a city and transitioning to a PWI located in a rural area was difficult for me. At the time, I was one of the only Latinas within my unit. Although I had received the same degree as some of my colleagues, I felt as if I did not belong at the institution and the surrounding area. The first 9 months in the job were incredibly difficult and I isolated myself often. Upon reflection, I can identify that isolation was a coping mechanism I used to protect myself as I navigated a new political climate and learned who to trust. I experienced imposter syndrome and constantly questioned if I had made the right decision in my job search. This dynamic made me question if I would be considered for higher level positions in the future.

Due to the limited amount of staff of color on campus, students of color consistently go to the same staff members when they need help. As someone who wholeheartedly loves working with students and fully believes in their capacity, I was often working long hours continuously and experienced burnout. It was difficult to simultaneously juggle the institution's expectations of me along with the needs of my students. I quickly learned to find my voice and found myself challenging other administrators on their viewpoints to provide the appropriate resources for students. However, over time I could connect closely with staff members who had similar experiences and were able to provide guidance while navigating the institution.

These colleagues quickly became my friends and were my support system both on and off campus.

As time continues to pass, I notice that more of my colleagues are leaving the field of student affairs. I considered leaving the field at times to become a mental health provider as I fully enjoy working with students on an individual basis and have a background in psychology. Working closely with students has made me realize the overwhelming gap in mental health providers that come underrepresented populations, especially communities that view mental health as taboo. I intend to stay in student affairs and try to see how I can integrate a more counseling based role in the future.

Marcus Emmanuelle Scales

As a first generation, Black male college student from a working class, single mother-headed household, education was always instilled as a priority. Early in my life, I was interested in professions that had financially lucrative rewards. First, I wanted to be a doctor after encountering a book, *The Pact*, about three Black men and their journeys to become doctors. Then in high school, I took an interest in computer science and wanted to be a computer engineer. Later as I began college, I developed an interest in business and ultimately graduated with a Bachelor of Science in business administration degree. However, during my senior year, I realized that I did not want to go into corporate America and none of my previous interests for a career spoke to my passion. The experiences of being a community assistant, president of the Black cultural society, and a member of Alpha Phi Alpha Fraternity, Incorporated at Bloomsburg University played a significant role in my career change to student affairs.

With Bloomsburg University having a fairly new student affairs graduate program, I explored the opportunity to enter the field and was impressed by what the program had to offer—a unique blend of counseling and student affairs. The instructional makeup of this program has significantly contributed to how I engage my students as a professional. The skill set learned from the fusion of these two helping professions has allowed me to connect with students on a deep and insightful level.

Beginning my career in the field at a Historically Black College/University (HBCU) provided a strong foundation in the purpose of my work. The environment at the institution was challenging, supportive, and culturally affirming. A familial presence permeated the institution on all levels because of the cultural dynamics and limited resources, collaboration was commonplace. In my second professional position, this time at a PWI in a rural part of New York State, a cultural shift accompanied my geographical adjustment. The environment seemed more siloed than what I had previously experienced. I questioned whether I made the right decision in leaving that comfortable environment to this unknown one. "Did I go from being celebrated to being tolerated?" was a question I asked myself. The political nature of the campus environment was evident from the very beginning and I had to learn quickly the rules to play or, as I believed, I would not survive.

Serving students of color at a PWI is extremely different, as both students and professionals look to you for insight to help solve institutional problems. There is a constant battle between advocating for students and being an agent of the institution. One false move can leave you in a position where students no longer see you as an ally or the institution is no longer in need of your services. I debate leaving the profession, seeing the frustrations of my peers, predecessors, and mainstays of the field; but I know students and particularly, students of color, need professionals who can relate to and advocate for them at higher education institutions. Those who have both public and private agendas against their interests will be ambitious, so those of us who can fight for them must be just as, if not more, ambitious. The desire to advocate for historically marginalized communities is a high priority for me and I love the field of education. The field of student affairs allows me to do both; so at this moment, I see myself persevering through the challenges the field brings because these communities need it. My interest in business remains strong as well; therefore, I have and will continue to explore the possibility of aligning those two interests while establishing myself as an agent of change in the realm of student affairs.

RECOMMENDATIONS

Based on our personal and professional experiences, we have compiled recommendations for both newer professionals of color and institutions to effectively support and provide career growth and advancement while honoring our identities.

Support from Institution, Department, Office, and Managers

Like students, new professionals can benefit from both challenge and support from the institution, department, and direct supervisors. Professionals will need a lot of support transitioning into their role, whether it be consistent in-person meetings, personal and professional support from their supervisor, or coaching to better understand the campus culture they must learn to navigate. Along with supporting new professionals, supervisors should encourage their supervisees to pursue their passions and to experience different functional areas within the field. Supporting a supervisee includes volunteer roles within the department and opportunities to collaborate with others outside of their functional area. Having the support of your supervisor as a new professional can be integral to developing both your professional identity and area of interest for your next position. Additionally, having the "I shine, you shine" mentality while supervising professionals of color helps to prove that you are working to make sure both you and your new employee are respected within your division.

Professional Development and Associations

At a PWI where there are not many professionals of color, there are, however, other networks to connect with that can support your work and help you stay resilient in the field. Professional associations including American College Personnel Association (ACPA) and National Association of Student Personnel Administrators (NASPA) are the largest associations that help professionals find connections with peers, colleagues, and mentors on other campuses. There are also smaller networks (e.g., regions, networks, coalitions, communities of practice, and knowledge communities) within these associations that provide a community. Within the field, there are also functional area specific associations that provide development and community, including the Association of College and University Housing Officers-International (ACUHO-I), Association of Fraternity/Sorority Advisors (AFA), National Association for Campus Activities (NACA), National Orientation Directors Association (NODA), and more.

Specifically for professionals of color, there are a few associations that provide community and education for scholar-practitioners as well as racial equity institutes, including the National Conference on Race and Ethnicity (NCORE) and Social Justice Training Institute (SJTI). These two associations are great ways for professionals of colors and allies to learn more about how they can affect change on campuses while learning more about how their personal identities fit into their work. Lastly, for scholar practitioners, the American Educational Research Association (AERA) and the Association on the Study of Higher Education (ASHE) are great ways to find support and further professional development with publications, pursuing the faculty route, and more.

Coalition Amongst Colleagues

In our experience as younger professionals, one of the most powerful tools for keeping us at our institution has been finding a powerful network of colleagues. While living in a rural area, it can be difficult to find others who share similar experiences as you. Finding other professionals at your institution with whom you connect can create a positive experience. Your network of colleagues can serve as both your safety net and with whom you can get a challenge when needed. We are fortunate to work with individuals who genuinely care about each other at the workplace and in their personal lives. It is important that new professionals find out how to build their network to seek advice on how to transition to the institution and to gain insight into the political culture.

Additionally, as you create your network at your current institution, it is valuable to build your network outside of your workplace. This connection can include student affair professionals at other institutions or people from the community who do not work for the same institution. As a new professional, it is important to remember that your career is not your entire life. Be prepared to look for support outside of the workplace to provide space to recharge and focus on other aspects of your life.

Creating a space for both new and returning professionals at our institution is essential for the retention of staff of color at a PWI. The creation of colleague network groups allows new professionals to meet across departments and create connections that can further enhance future goals and job prospects. These colleague network groups create meetup events and professional development opportunities as well as help to advocate our needs and concerns to senior administration.

CONCLUSION

Being a professional of color at an elite PWI has a plethora of challenges and the work is not for the faint of heart. While we believe self-care and support are essential elements of survival, one must also be aware of the political nuances of the institutions at which they are attempting to make a change. Systemic and institutional change is a part of our responsibility as professionals of color. While these institutions may not have been built with us in mind, institutions are decorating their brochures with our faces. Therefore, we must make sure to hold them accountable for making campuses more culturally affirming and accessible.

REFERENCES

Evans, N. J., Forney, D. S., Guido, F. M., Patton, L. D., & Renn, K. A. (2009). *Student development in college: Theory, research, and practice* (2nd ed.). San Francisco, CA: Wiley.

Janosik, S. M., & Creamer, D. G. (2003). Introduction: A comprehensive model. In S. M. Janosik, D. G. Creamer, J. B. Hirt, R. B. Winston, S. A. Saunders, & D. L. Cooper (Eds.), *Supervising new professionals in student affairs* (pp. 1–16). New York, NY: Brunner-Routledge.

Magolda, M. B. B. (2008). Three elements of self-authorship. *Journal of College Student Development, 49*(4), 269–284.

Marshall, S. M., Gardner, M. M., Hughes, C., & Lowery, U. (2016). Attrition from student affairs: Perspectives from those who exited the profession. *Journal of Student Affairs Research and Practice, 53*(2), 146–159.

Renn, K. A., & Hodges, J. (2007). The first year on the job: Experiences of new professionals in student affairs. *NASPA journal, 44*(2), 367–391.

Torres, V., & Hernandez, E. (2007). The influence of ethnic identity on self-authorship: A longitudinal study of Latino/a college students. *Journal of College Student Development, 48*(5), 558–573.

Tull, A. (2006). Synergistic supervision, job satisfaction, and intention to turnover of new professionals in student affairs. *Journal of College Student Development, 47*(4), 465–480.

Winston, R. B., & Creamer, D. G. (1997). *Improving staffing affairs practices in student affairs.* San Francisco, CA: Jossey-Bass.

Winston, R. B., & Creamer, D. G. (1998). Staff supervision and professional development: An integrated approach. In W. A. Bryan & R. A. Schwartz (Eds.), *Strategies for staff development: Personal and professional education in the 21st century* (New Directions for Student Services, No. 84, pp. 29–42). San Francisco, CA: Jossey Bass.

CHAPTER 12

FROM AUDRE TO LAURYN

An Ode to Self-Care

Diana Morris
Vanderbilt University

Higher education, student affairs, and similarly focused graduate/professional programs generally provide foundational knowledge of the history of higher education and student development theory, but few address the realities of balancing the demands of the profession with the demands of being human. The absence of this structured conversation is noticeable, especially given the nature and demands of the work and the focus on self-care and wellness within the field. In this chapter, the author will provide personal examples of the stresses and threats that exist for student affairs professionals of color looking to survive and thrive in their roles as well as offer suggestions for recognizing and addressing pitfalls to self-care and well-being that can arise in the pursuit of success.

One look at the course listings of any higher education, student affairs, or similarly focused graduate/professional program provides insight into the knowledge and skills the industry deems important for success. Take, for example, some of the top programs in the country as listed by U.S. News

No Ways Tired, pages 105–110
Copyright © 2019 by Information Age Publishing
All rights of reproduction in any form reserved.

and World Report in 2017—their course catalogues center on the history of higher education, student development theory, organizational structures, and contemporary issues in the field (Michigan State University, 2017; Regents of The University of Michigan, 2017; University of Georgia College of Education, 2017; University of Maryland, 2015; University of Pennsylvania Graduate School of Education, 2017; *U.S. News & World Report*, 2017a; *U.S. News & World Report*, 2017b). While most programs have these common content areas, few offer coursework that provides concrete preparation for balancing the demands of the profession with the demands of being human. Admittedly, due to the range of experiences people can have when entering the field and the numerous directions they can take within it, this type of curriculum might be difficult to develop, but given the nature and demands of our work—especially within student affairs—the absence is noticeable. This gap is especially striking when one considers the ways the concept of balance is weaved throughout the very fabric of our industry, either as the subject of interview questions, conversations among colleagues, the focus of conference presentations, or resources offered to students.

As a second-year master's candidate preparing for the post-graduate job search, I made sure to have a firm grasp of my favorite theories and the ways my practicum positions and graduate assistantships would transfer into a future role. In interview after interview, I pulled from Sanford's (1966) notion of challenge and support to frame my professional philosophy and utilized the S.T.A.R. (situation, task, action, and result) method to describe my experiences. When the final questions hit, the ones about what I like to do for fun and how I achieve work–life balance, I felt relieved. That inquiry was easy to answer because I navigated stress and self-care all the time. In the instances where I felt overwhelmed with classes, work, and anything else life threw my way, I read, pretended to host a Food Network special, listened to music, ran, and traveled as far and wide as possible. These tools worked previously and I had no doubt they would continue to work as I entered a professional role.

When the interviews concluded and the offers were extended, I accepted a live-in, live-on position in residence life and made the solo journey to a brand-new city and way of life. The slower pace of campus during the summer gave me time to train my staff, prepare for students' arrival, and begin taking stock of how I would navigate the personal, professional, and political spaces of the institution in general and specifically as a Black woman. Previous experiences and observations had highlighted that the adage of being "twice as good" was a cliché for a reason and I understood that my words and actions might be under additional scrutiny from colleagues, students, parents, and other constituents no matter how seemingly benign. When the fall semester started, I felt confident in my role and was prepared to take on whatever came my way. Then, that November, I had my first on-call rotation.

During my interviews, I had expressed that being on-call was something I was looking forward to and it was true—with my sights on eventually holding a senior leadership position, I knew that experience with crisis response would give me a wide range of skills to pull from throughout my career. The first few days with the duty phone were relatively easy and calls ranged from maintenance issues and lockouts to low-level medical transports and support for student staff. That all changed when my colleague's name flashed on the display at around 2:00 a.m. one morning and, half-awake, I answered.

As I rushed across campus to where a student discovered the body of their roommate who died by suicide, I was fully alert and I remember a distinct ringing in my ears. In the moments immediately following that call—and all the calls that would come after—I knew exactly what to do as instinct kicked in. I spoke with students, spoke with parents, updated relevant personnel, wrote reports, sent emails, made phone calls, held office hours, and connected students to resources. Those minutes, hours, days, weeks, and months rolled into each other and it felt as if I was on autopilot. When I was not in my office, I was with a staff member; when I was not with a staff member, I was with a student; and when I was not with a student, I was in a meeting with a colleague, faculty member, or campus partner. The workdays were long and the task list never seemed to get shorter, but there was a job to do and it was imperative that I do it well and before I knew it, I was entering the final stretch of my second year in the position.

When speaking with people outside of the university setting about my job, I never really went into too much detail. After all, working in housing—and student affairs in general—is something that is hard to understand unless you experience it firsthand. Even as I was living the experience, I was still learning what it meant to always be "on" and to engage in emotional labor at what felt like all hours of the day. Hochschild conceptualized emotional labor as the expectation for "mothering" that "silently attaches itself to many a job description" (as cited in Schaubroeck & Jones, 2000, p. 168) and Brotheridge and Grandey (2002) further delineated this labor into two categories: job-focused (i.e., the level of emotional demands a position requires) and employee-focused (i.e., the way an individual manages their emotions as they meet the demands of a position). I did not realize it at the time, but this unspoken job requirement was the defining feature of my position and everything that came with it.

When people asked if I enjoyed my job, I answered that it depended on the minute and it was as honest of a response as I could give. There were moments when I could easily identify highlights and moments of fulfillment and joy and others where I struggled to give voice to the feelings of exhaustion, toxicity, and disconnect that cast a shadow on what I did. As those struggles increased, I knew that I needed to remove myself from the situation, but there always seemed to be an excuse to stay. I drafted a resignation letter in January that I never sent. I watched for vacancies in other offices and institutions. I even helped individuals transition out of the environment and into other opportunities, but I returned each day because, in my mind, there was so much more that I could—and needed—to do for the students I served and for the colleagues left in the trenches with me.

Eventually, the decision to stay or leave was made for me. That April, my colleagues and I received notice that the department was restructuring and our position would be dissolved at the end of the semester. Although I hid it well, the news was a blow to my professional confidence and my mental reserve. After all, it is not every day that you find out you have one month to find a job and a place to live, all while devoting time and energy to the job you already have. However, as I navigated the situation then and as I look back on it now, this experience provided an invaluable lesson—as well as I treat other people, I must treat myself just as well as I treat other people, if not better, because no one else can, or will, do that for me.

No one explicitly asked me to blur the lines between who I was as a person and who I was as a staff member—I chose to do that. I *watched* myself do that because my definition of success was one where the benefit to others eclipsed the benefit to myself. The letter outlining the department's new structure was a crash course in learning that things will move forward with or without me.

As I officially started job searching, I re-evaluated my priorities and worked to adjust the scales so things balanced more in my favor. I looked around and saw the amazing support system I had among friends, family, and mentors. I pursued positions in environments that better aligned with my professional and personal standards. I threw out the playbook of what works when I am feeling overwhelmed and began to identify what me being "overwhelmed" even looks like. Most importantly, I redefined what I considered strength and success.

Before being laid off, strength and success meant keeping my head down and getting the work done. If something happened, I let myself sit with it for a minute—maybe two—and then I pushed it down and kept moving forward. This employee-focused emotional labor allowed me to do my job, but it was a horrible strategy—hypocritical at best and unsustainable at worst. For all the empathy I showed others, I had little for myself and for all the resources I directed other people to, I never took the time to consider that they were available to me as well.

When I went through interviews as a graduate student, I thought I knew what it meant to balance my life and my work. I understood the concept of making sure I do not pour from an empty cup. I paid just enough attention in my undergraduate psychology class and during flights to see the connection between the flight attendant's words about oxygen masks and making sure that I am okay before I try to help others. I also listened to enough

Lauryn Hill (1998) to know her wise counsel of "how you gon' win if you ain't right within" by heart. However, this was all a theoretical, romanticized understanding of self-care and well-being. The experiences leading up to this moment showed me that operationalizing these concepts into sustainable, day-to-day practice was a different story. After all, haven't we all given advice that we ourselves find difficult to follow? Aren't there things we know to be true for others, but we don't necessarily realize they apply to us, too? Nearly all my training prepared me to be of service for others, but along the way, I forgot to be of service to myself.

Gilkes described the tightrope navigated by professional Black women as being "caught in a possible conflicting web of expectations which are far more complex than those of simply being a professional, being a woman, or being Black" (as cited in Bell, 1990, p. 460) and I am intimately aware of this reality. During this period of my career, I worked double time to meet the demands of the job in front of me and the multiple—at times, contradictory—needs of the constituents around me, all at the expense of my emotional and physical health and my personal and mental well-being. I know the "mothering" that is inherent in our field is simultaneously amplified and muted by the racial (Black) and gender (woman) identities I inhabit, causing me to enter a cycle of pouring from my cup until it was drained, all the while biting my tongue lest I be perceived as aggressive, combative, or worse, unable to perform. I was, in effect, hyper-visible and invisible at the same time, and in the end, none of the dexterity I possessed mattered. As Audre Lorde (1984) mused in a space and context different from this, but no less relevant, my silence did not protect me. I now know that "caring for myself is not self-indulgence, it is self-preservation, and that is an act of political warfare" (Lorde, 1988, p. 131). As a professional in the field, especially a professional of color and even more as a professional Black woman, self-preservation and self-care are a reality that few textbooks cover, but one that must be acknowledged.

I am thankful to know now that it is okay not to be okay and that it is okay to redefine what "okay" looks like. In fact, this continuous redefining is critical to ensuring my preservation in an environment that requires so much. I began my career thinking I had a firm grasp on what I needed to be happy and fulfilled in my professional and, by extension, personal life. However, the stressors, tests, and non-negotiables I experienced as a graduate student and early in my career journey are very different than those I will experience as my career continues. I had to rebrand resiliency and accept that it is just as much about acknowledging that something is wrong as it is about making it to the other side. I had to remember that accepting that I cannot do it all is not the same as saying I cannot do anything at all or a sign of failure. Just as I helped other people identify the areas of decay they should cut from their lives, I now know to respect and trust myself enough to act on those areas when they reveal themselves in my own life. It does no one any good to become a martyr and push myself to the breaking point. The nature of our work may subtly ask for that, but it is okay to decline taking on that role. As I continue through my career, whether it be in student affairs or beyond, these lessons will continue to make themselves known and it is important that I remain willing to learn.

REFERENCES

Bell, E. L. (1990). The bicultural life experience of career-oriented Black women. *Journal of Organizational Behavior, 11*(6), 459–477.

Brotheridge, C. M., & Grandey, A. A. (2002). Emotional labor and burnout: Comparing two perspectives of "people work." *Journal of Vocational Behavior, 60,* 17–39.

Hill, L. (1998, July 7). Doo wop (that thing). On *The miseducation of Lauryn Hill* [CD]. New York, NY: Columbia Records.

Lorde, A. (1984). *Sister outsider: Essays and speeches.* Berkeley, CA: Crossing Press.

Lorde, A. (1988). *A burst of light.* Ann Arbor, MI: Firebrand Books.

Michigan State University. (2017). Master of arts in higher, adult, and lifelong education program requirements. *College of Education Department of Educational Administration.* Retrieved from http://education.msu.edu/ead/hale/masters/progplan.asp

Regents of The University of Michigan. (2017). Master's degree in higher education requirements. *University of Michigan School of Education.* Retrieved from http://www.soe.umich.edu/academics/masters_programs/he/he_requirements/

Sanford, N. (1966). *Self and society.* New York, NY: Atherton Press.

Schaubroeck, J., & Jones, J. (2000). Antecedents of workplace emotional labor dimensions and moderators of their effects on physical symptoms. *Journal of Organizational Behavior, 21*(2), 163–183.

University of Georgia College of Education. (2017). PhD in counseling and student personnel services (college student affairs administration). *Department of Counseling and Human Development Services.* Retrieved from https://coe.uga.edu/academics/degrees/phd/counseling-student-personnel-service

University of Maryland. (2015). Student Affairs (HISA). *The Graduate School Catalogue 2017–2018.* Retrieved from http://apps.gradschool.umd.edu/Catalog/public-programs-detail.php?HISA#Courses

University of Pennsylvania Graduate School of Education. (2017). Program of student—Core requirements. *Penn GSE—Higher education division.* Retrieved from https://www.gse.upenn.edu/hed/msed

U.S. News & World Report. (2017a). Best higher education administration programs. *U.S. News & World Report best grad schools rankings.* Retrieved from https://www.usnews.com/best-graduate-schools/top-education-schools/higher-education-administration-rankings

U.S. News & World Report. (2017b). Best student counseling programs. *U.S. News & World Report best grad schools rankings.* Retrieved from https://www.usnews.com/best-graduate-schools/top-education-schools/student-counseling-rankings

CHAPTER 13

WHERE DO WE GO FROM HERE

Joi Sampson
Mercy College

This chapter looks at some of the challenges Black women student affairs professionals experience while working in predominantly White institutions and how these challenges are tied to issues with race and power. Relating to scholarly literature, I will use my personal narrative as a Black woman working in higher education to discuss my experiences with identity, isolation, and microaggressions and offer recommendations.

Higher education has a long dark history when it comes to matters of race. The African slave trade was a source of economic prosperity for the academy during the 18th century, helping to bring well-known institutions such as Harvard, William and Mary, and Columbia into great wealth and prestige (Wilder, 2013). All the while, African slaves were viewed with a lens of servitude. This view would not begin to shift until more than two decades later. Eventually, the educational systems in America would be challenged to rethink how they dealt with matters of race. Two examples include such landmark cases like *Plessy v. Ferguson* (1896) in which the Supreme Court

No Ways Tired, pages 111–118
Copyright © 2019 by Information Age Publishing
All rights of reproduction in any form reserved.

ruled in favor of segregation under the notion of separate but equal and *Brown v. Board of Education* (1952) in which the court unanimously ruled against segregation citing it was harmful to African American students.

In 1965, President Lyndon Johnson signed the Higher Education Act (HEA) into law with the goal of equalizing education. In addition to the implementation of funds that would provide economically disadvantaged students access to education, the HEA carried with it a hiring mandate. To continue receiving federal funding, colleges were expected to hire more African American or Black people to serve in greater capacity at their institutions (Smith, 1978). Without clarity for this new federal mandate, institutions were left to form their own interpretation. As a result, the capacities in which Black people served in higher education left much-needed reform. When hired, Blacks filled positions with low-level status (i.e., custodians and cooks) and were paid lower wages than their White counterparts, which was especially true for Black women. As the hiring of Blacks moved beyond low-level positions in higher education, Smith (1978) reported those within this group were usually hired as staff officers—those who rely on the need to share information or influence to line officers to change or implement an idea without authority—rather than line officers—managers with administrative authority who directly supervise staff and manage budgets who are given the authority to make decisions.

Black women often find themselves concentrated in lower-level administrative positions, carrying out policy rather than formulating policy (Crawford & Smith, 2005). Black women are further plagued with adversity because of their gender in addition to race. Scholars have coined two terms that represent the multifaceted disparities experienced by the Black women because of their race and their gender—the double burden (St. Jean & Feagin, 1998) and double jeopardy (Jones-Thomas, Witherspoon, & Speight, 2008). Mosely (1980) further asserts that Black women are an "endangered species" (p. 296), illustrating the lack of upward mobility Black women have access to in predominantly White institutions (PWI). This lack of mobility is an unofficial classification for institutions that suggests rights are inherent to Whites (Bourke, 2016), which is stalling the progress of Black women in higher education and thus, eliminating their presence in critical ways.

The experiences and challenges that racial minority groups, particularly Black women professionals, working at PWIs endure can make it hard for them to take hold of the principles and model the idea that hard work will pay off. I believe many racial and ethnic minority groups start out with a belief they can be successful in whatever they do; however, it is only after adverse experiences that the systemic forms of power and oppression are revealved and they become enlightened, feeling the burden of operating with this new knowledge.

THE FORMATION OF A DOUBLE-CONSCIOUSNESS

My first paid position in higher education came when I was an undergraduate student. I had a federal work-study job at my institution's career and employment office. This student employment position gave me my first up close and personal look at a professional office in academia. I worked closely with the career counseling staff and although none of the three female career counselors looked like me racially, I developed an admiration for their professionalism and expertise. They looked powerful in their suits and each one had her own office. I often thought, "This is what I want for my future"—to dress in a power suit every day and have an office to call my own. Working at the center became an exciting time for me as I was developing an understanding of what I wanted to do with the rest of my life— what Baxter Magolda (2008) refers to as self-authorship. By this time, I was still unaware of the role race and gender would play in my career journey.

Much of the training in my work-study position came from one of the counselors, a White woman working at the college on a part-time basis. She oriented me to the routine work and daily operations, enabling me to support office projects. She also sought to "train" me on what I perceived as how to be more refined—including proper etiquette when interacting with office visitors. Accepting the idea that I was unskilled in many areas and in need of weekly training/refinement tutorials from my White supervisor, I launched a personal analytical examination of my life to determine areas that entailed the "unskilled" woman I saw myself to be in the eyes of my supervisor. The list of deficits I created because of my examination made me begin to live with apology, like Blacks often feel they need to do. Suppressing the "deficit" parts of my life, I seldom spoke about growing up in the South Bronx or talked about the public schools I attended. For fear of sounding unintelligent in front of anyone who was outside of the Black community, I began code-switching, "an act of racial compromise for African American English users..." (Krichevsky, 2015, p. 235). I worked hard to eliminate the use of "Black" vernacular when around Whites. In essence, I tried to strip myself of my Black identity to fit into what seemed acceptable by "White standards" according to what I was learning.

I have since come to understand the way I thought about myself through the eyes of my White supervisor was what W. E. B. Du Bois called the double-consciousness or the concept of two-ness as the world only allows Blacks be seen through the revelation of the other world and not through their self-consciousness. He poetically illustrated the internal struggle I experienced in the 1903 text, *The Souls of Black Folk,*

> It is a particular sensation, this double-consciousness, this sense of always looking at one's self through the eyes of others, of measuring one's soul by

the tape of a world that looks on in amused contempt and pity. One ever fills his two-ness,—an American, a Negro; two souls, two thoughts, two unreconciled strivings; two waring ideals in one dark body whose dogged strength alone keeps it from being torn asunder. (p. 2)

While looking to change myself for the sake of my PWI, I would choose to deny my Black identity. Although ever conscious of my race, I carried that feeling of two-ness Dubois speaks about and it infiltrated every sector of my professional life. By the time I completed graduate school, I felt that I reached more of my goals related to shifting my identity. I became the professional with the characteristics I admired in the career counselors I worked with as an undergraduate student. Once I secured full-time work, I learned that my previous efforts to conform to a predominantly White academic environment did not exclude me from facing challenges because of my race. My first post-graduate employment experience would teach me more about what it meant to be a Black woman working in the field of higher education than my entire graduate program did about the profession itself.

BEING INVISIBLE

It was an exciting feeling to secure my first full-time professional job after graduate school. I felt ready and equipped with my master's degree in hand to take on the world of academia. I took a position as an academic advisor at a small proprietary school, which could also be classified as a PWI. In this new position, I was eager to put all I learned into practice. I worked long hours, volunteered for extra duties and responsibilities, and regularly attended events to network. It was my belief that in doing these things, I would secure a place for myself at the head of the advancement line. I sincerely thought that if I worked hard and gave my all to the position, I would be rewarded with promotions and salary increases. It was a foolproof formula: Hard work + Diligence + Self-Sacrifice = Promotion and Salary Increase (PPS).

According to Sanchez-Hucles and Davis (2010), African American women are more likely "to experience unfair treatment in training and advancement, disengagement, discrimination, prejudice, and lack of psychosocial and instrumental support" (p. 174). However, I did not realize that I was working from what felt like a deficit position the entire time and no matter how many events I attended or how many late nights I worked, being a woman of color became like an anchor that was holding me down. I watched my White colleagues, who were doing some of the same things as I, move at a faster rate of advancement. In the less than five years I spent employed at the institution, I watched two of my White colleagues be promoted almost a total of five times between them. I was promoted zero times. I was, however, in time dubbed with a new title—"Administrator-in-charge." From the outside it sounded important, yet it bore little to no authority and was used only during evening shifts after all other administrators had gone home for the evening. What I experienced was indeed working from a deficit position—one that is a common occurrence as "Black women administrators are, for the most part, invisible beings. They are isolated and their academic opportunities are limited by barriers that have nothing to do with their preparation, qualifications, or competency" (Mosley, 1980, p. 306).

For a long time, I gave excuses for my immobility in the workplace, largely finding fault within myself. I was convinced that if I were smarter, more punctual, more articulate, and maybe friendlier, I could have been promoted just as my White counterparts were. While I began to try a quick fix on myself, I started to see other issues at hand after learning my White supervisor went into my office one morning before I arrived and looked through my things under the guise of "looking for a document." She left many of my papers disheveled and my desk drawer opened. This experience awakened me. The sense of disrespect and violation helped me to see that the issues with mobility had less to do with my perceived inadequacies and more to do with a lack of respect for who I was as a professional.

Another challenge I experienced as a new professional of color working in higher education was not being taken seriously. The position I held was a very visible one as it involved mentoring students, facilitating workshops, organizing orientations, and collaborating with other offices on projects in addition to providing academic advising to students. While I was well liked by my students, that same attitude was not translated to me by some of my colleagues. The offices assistants in my department regularly questioned any direct orders I gave them which included requests to make copies, call students, locate files, and other related tasks. The office assistants who were non-Black minorities never blatantly protested my instructions, but they would do things that relayed reluctances in their follow through including becoming quizzical regarding directives and double checking my orders with others, including my superiors. When these tactics were unsuccessful, the office assistant would simply delay in carrying out my requests, sometimes to the point of not meeting time-sensitive deadlines. These tactics felt demeaning; however, it did not stop at the administrative assistant level. My direct supervisor also challenged my abilities on several occasions and would micromanage my work as if to assume I would predictably miss a detail. Such behaviors felt unwarranted when I received positive evaluations at each yearly performance review. In my interactions with my supervisor, I noticed that when I made suggestions or had any requests, she was slow to take action or respond. Initially, her sluggishness to implement or acknowledge my ideas appeared to be attributed to thoughtfulness and strategizing as if she needed to carefully consider the things I shared. Yet, it was likely more closely attributed to the tendency for persons who are members of the dominant societal group to at times show a rejection of knowledge or authority from persons from racially-ethnic minority groups. Delgado and Stefancic (2017) identify the behaviors of subtle rejection or undermining of persons of color as a microaggression. The authors state,

> Microaggressions can be thought of as small acts of racism, consciously or unconsciously perpetrated, welling up from the assumptions about racial matters most of us absorb from the cultural heritage in which we come of age in the United States. (p. 2)

In an implicit association test given to groups of Americans to measure their social cognition toward groups different from their own, it was found that participants harbored negative attitudes toward minorities, foreigners, [and] women (Delgado & Stefancic, 2017). Such studies support critical race theory (CRT) that exposes a correlation between decision-making, group dynamics, self-interest, emotion, and other factors associated with race and privilege/power. As student affairs professionals, we have had to manage many of these factors in our institutions and look for ways to challenge them as "Whiteness must be challenged where it exists; regardless of the social organization in which it can manifest itself (universities, corporation, schools...) those committed to racial equality must develop a personal practice to challenge it" (Bonilla-Silva, 2003, p. 184).

RECOMMENDATIONS

"African Americans use a variety of coping strategies for racism including... overachieving or being overly successful, praying and using positive thinking, having the ability to laugh at situations, and relying on social support" (Jones Thomas et al., p. 309). There are two strategies I have employed as a Black woman student affairs professional to help me find the strength to challenge racial disparity and maintain my mental wellness. The first strategy has been to build a network of allies—other professionals who can provide encouragement and support, especially during heightened times of implicit racial tensions. Once, stricken with tears, I had to go into a bathroom stall and call one of my allies. She, in turn, helped me get through an emotional situation and move forward with the workday. The thing to be careful about when utilizing an ally is not to succumb to the temptation to merely gossip about colleagues or the institution. The relationship should be there to help teach us how to deal with situations that arise. I have found some of my most cherished allies were individuals who have been employed at the institution longer than I have and therefore, have a healthy understanding of institutional culture. The second group of allies might be those who are members of the same racial group who can be essential but not exclusive and they can also come from other minority racial groups or White, non-Hispanic groups. However, for a White person to make a good ally for a person of color, Paul Kivel suggested. "[White people] . . . need to listen carefully to the voices of people of color so that [they] understand and give credence to their experience" (Rothenberg, 2012, p. 158). While I cannot say that I have had the experience of connecting with a White, non-Hispanic ally, I have had the occasional White colleague or superior who was concerned with my well-being and acclimation to the institution. Although they proved supportive and helpful, I did not feel the relationship reached a level of comfortability in which I could address matters of racial discrimination nor did they inquire to see if racial discrimination was something I was experiencing.

The second strategy that has helped me deal with racial disparity has been to adopt a mentor. Research has shown that Black women thrive in their careers when they have mentorship. According to Crawford (2005), "Mentoring would give African American female administrators greater responsibility and visibility and would encourage young African Americans to choose higher education as a career" (p. 53). In a study cited by Jean-Marie, Williams, and Sherman (2009) in which they examined the experiences of Black women educational leaders, the participants reported the keys to their success included, "exceeding performance expectations, communicating effectively, connecting with mentors, building positive relationships with managers and colleagues and using their cultural backgrounds to enhance job performance" (p. 567).

Choosing a mentor should be done with care. A mentor can be a former instructor from a previously attended institution or an instructor that teaches at the institution where you are currently employed. As a suggestion, an ideal mentor for a student affairs professional will be someone who has some experience in the field of higher education and has shown themselves to be successful contributors to the profession.

CONCLUSION

There is no quick resolution or panacea for eradicating the ills of racism, hegemony, or employment disparity for persons of color. However, there are people who have the power to contribute to solutions for change by using their voices to combat injustices, teach others to be aware that the issues exist, help those who have been and continue to be negatively affected by the issues, and find appropriate methods to bring about change.

In addition, those in positions of power must be encouraged to see racism as a pervasive part of our society and not allow it to persist in our institutions of higher education.

REFERENCES

Baxter Magolda, M. (2008). Three elements of self-authorship. *Journal of College Student Development, 49*(4), 269–284.

Bonilla-Silva, E. (2003). *Racism without racist.* Lanham, MD: Rowman & Littlefield.

Bourke, B. (2016). Meaning and implications of being labelled a predominantly White institution. *College and University, 91*(3), 12–21.

Crawford, K., & Smith, D. (2005). The we and the us: Mentoring African American women. *Journal of Black Studies, 36*(1), 52–67.

Delgado, R., & Stefancic, J. (2017). *Critical race theory: An introduction.* New York: New York University Press.

Du Bois, W. E. B. (1994). *The souls of Black folk.* New York, NY: Dover.

Jean-Marie, G., Williams, V., & Sherman, S. (2009). Black women's leadership experiences: Examining the intersectionality of race and gender. *Advances in Human Development, 11*(5), 562–581.

Jones-Thomas, A., Witherspoon, K., & Speight, S. (2008). Gendered racism, psychological distress, and coping styles of African American women. *Cultural Diversity and Ethnic Minority Psychology, 14*(4), 307–314.

Krichevsky, J. (2015). Other people's English: Code-meshing, code-switching, and African American literacy. *Composition Studies, 43*(2), 234–237.

Mosley, H. M. (1980). Black women administrators in higher education: An endangered species. *Journal of Black Studies, 10*(3), 295–310.

Rothenberg, S. P. (2012). *White privilege: Essential readings on the other side of racism.* New York, NY: Worth.

Sanchez-Hucles, J., & Davis, D. (2010). Women and women of color in leadership: Complexity, identity, and intersectionality. *American Psychologist, 65*(3), 171–181.

Smith, H. C. (1978). The peculiar status of Black administrators in educational institutions. *Journal of Negro Education, 47*(4), 323–327.

St. Jean, Y., & Feagin, J. (1998). *Double burden: Black women and everyday racism.* Armonk, New York, NY: M.E. Sharpe.

Wilder, C. S. (2013). *Ebony & ivy: Race, slavery, and the troubled history of America's universities.* New York, NY: Bloomsbury Press.

CHAPTER 14

FORCED TO DECIDE

Being Visible and Resilient Against Colonization

Charlie A. Scott (Diné)
University of Denver

The history of education has always been violent to Indigenous thought(s) and knowledge(s). The origins of post-secondary institutions catered towards European-Americans that did not initially include Indigenous Peoples. Education was and continues to be an apparatus of violence towards Indigenous Peoples. Yet, Indigenous Peoples challenge and disrupt that violence through their own ancestral strength(s) and connections as they move towards resisting settler colonial logics in higher education. Indigenous Peoples are forced to decide between being rendered invisible or visibly challenging settler colonial logics.

It is the middle of September, the first day of my job at The University of Rhode Island, and I am exploring the rooms of the building trying to get a feel of the place outside of my office. I enter a room and see this giant flag framed and encased on a wall. It is not a typical U.S. flag. Rather, the flag belongs to the Narragansett Indian Tribe, the closest and only federally

No Ways Tired, pages 119–128
Copyright © 2019 by Information Age Publishing
All rights of reproduction in any form reserved.

recognized Indigenous community within what is currently known as "Rhode Island." I was momentarily surprised by the flag's presence because it was the only indication, and still continues to be the only indication, of the local Indigenous community. This circumstance is the opposite of what I was used to while growing while growing up in the central part of the Navajo Nation. I was used to seeing my nation's flag on every pole alongside the flags of the United States and Arizona, but seeing other Indigenous communities' flags was and is a rarity, especially on college and university campuses.

Indigenous Peoples within what is currently known as the "United States" have a complex and inherently violent relationship with education. Memories of American Indian boarding schools, children removal, and exploitative archeologists and anthropologists haunt the grandparents of many Indigenous youth. Yet, these narratives of violence are not thoroughly mentioned within academia. These histories of educational violence towards Indigenous Peoples are often ignored throughout education, whether K–12 or higher education. Across the "United States," only a handful of non-tribal colleges and universities recognize that they are on stolen land or are prepared to interrogate the settler colonial logics within their environment. Logics that often silence and erase Indigenous Peoples; both of which are themes that I have become quite intimate with since leaving the Navajo Nation in 2013. Yet, despite the attempted silencing and erasure, many Indigenous Peoples, myself included, have developed and are developing mechanisms and means of survival and strength for restoring and reclaiming spaces denied to them, historically and presently. All of which is aspiring and preparing for an indigenized future.

Throughout this chapter, the phrase *Indigenous Peoples* will be used as the more contemporary, political, and inclusive term to refer to all who identify as American Indians, Native Americans, Alaskan Natives, and/or Natives. The term *Indigenous* refers to a group of peoples who have specific ancestral connections to a "particular place before any outside peoples were introduced to the lands" (Brayboy, Fann, Castagno, & Solyom, 2012, p. 4). One definition for Indigenous Peoples is that they "are those who have creation stories, not colonization stories, about how we/they came to a particular place—indeed how we/they came to be a place" (Tuck & Yang, 2012, p. 6). Native Hawaiians and Alaskan Natives are included in the term Indigenous Peoples. It is important to note that their histories with education are unique and complex, which is common among many indigenous communities across the world. Additionally, it is essential to reject the monolithic identity that has been historically used when referencing Indigenous Peoples, whether in research, data, scholarship, historical documents, and more. This is achieved by continuously adding the "s" on the end of any phrases that refer to Indigenous Peoples. In addition, it is important to capitalize the "i" in Indigenous and the "p" in Peoples,

Indigenous Peoples, as a form of respect and to recognize the sovereignty of Indigenous Peoples. Indigenous Peoples are diverse and have their own stories of creation and sense of being.

I am someone who was born and raised near the red mesas and juniper trees of my Diné (Navajo) ancestors. My experiences as a Diné are quite different than someone who grew up within the Narragansett Indian Tribe. My community did not experience illegal "detribalization," which happened with the Narragansett Indian Tribe during 1880–1884. In addition, our stories of creation differ in how we came to a place and how we became a place. It is important to acknowledge and recognize why certain terms are privileged over others.

Settler colonialism is an ideological structure that regulates the everyday lives of colonized peoples through settler colonial logics. Louis Althusser (1971) described ideology as "systems of ideas and representations which dominate the mind of a man or a social group" (p. 158). These "systems of ideas" are informed and developed by a larger ideological framework that affects the development of representations and the creation of reality. Maile Arvin (Kanaka Maoli), Eve Tuck (Unangax and Aleut), and Angie Morrill (Klamath) argued in *Decolonizing Feminism: Challenging Connections Between Settler Colonialism and Heteropatriarchy* (Arvin, Tuck, & Morrill, 2013) that settler colonialism "is a persistent social and political formation in which newcomers/colonizers/settlers come to a place, claim it as their own, and do whatever it takes to disappear the Indigenous [P]eoples that are there" (p. 12). The distinction of settler colonialism is that there is an intentional construction of "a new home on the land, a homemaking that insists on settler sovereignty" (Tuck & Yang, 2012, p. 5). In *Toward a Tribal Critical Race Theory in Education*, Brayboy (2006), a Lumbee scholar, described colonialism as a cyclical reinforcement of settler colonial thought(s), knowledge(s), and (mis)understandings of power. Settler colonialism reproduces violence against Indigenous Peoples every day because of the continuous occupation of settlers. Settler colonialism informs the social and the political, which is the most active existence Indigenous Peoples whose identities reflect a socio-political positionality. Indigenous Peoples are recognized sovereign nations by the "United States," though arguably limited. Thus, Indigenous Peoples possessed a unique process of racialization. Indigenous Peoples' very socio-political identity is garnished through a settler colonial imagination, regulated and informed by the logics of settler colonialism, which is most apparent in the history of educating Indigenous Peoples.

The premise of education towards Indigenous Peoples has always been forced assimilation and violent acculturation of European-American thought(s) and behavior(s). From the late eighteenth century to the early twentieth century, Indigenous youth were forced to attend American Indian boarding schools to "uplift them from a state of savagery to an exalted plane of civilization" (Okihiro, 2016, p. 95), in which they contributed to the developing nationhood of the "United States." Through the developing nationhood, Indigenous communities were displaced as the "United States" waged war and violence against them for its desire for expansion and sovereignty. Education became weaponized and used as a tool of assimilation into European-American culture for Indigenous youth during this period of development. The history of student affairs professionals intertwines with that very history of assimilation through education. The seminal documents, *The Student Personnel Point of View* (American Council on Education, 1937) and the revised 1949 edition, promoted the tenacity of education is geared towards preserving, transmitting, and enriching "culture" through scholarship, instruction, and research. The revised 1949 edition further posited that the individual is a "responsible participant in the societal processes of American democracy" (American Council on Education, 1949, p. 18). Education was then a space of preparation for the development of American "culture" and the indoctrination of American politics. Colleges and universities had a political responsibility to maintain the faith of the individual in the democratic state of America. James (2004) further argued that "the structures and procedures of higher education flow from, build on, and reinforce the values, norms, identities and status systems of the mainstream majority" (p. 50). Higher education was and continues to be an apparatus of American colonization and displacement of Indigenous Peoples, simply by committing to the preservation, transmission, and enrichment of American "culture." Both the 1937 and revised 1949 edition of *The Student Personnel Point of View* highlighted the amalgamation of the political and social that are integral to the philosophy of American education and its preservation.

As an emerging practitioner in student affairs, I struggle with navigating higher education because of its direct lineage with settler colonialism. The very premise of higher education is preparing students to be responsible participants in American democracy (American Council on Education, 1949). The history of higher education portrays how violent the space was and continues to be against myself, my ancestors, and many other Indigenous Peoples. How I engage with the settler colonial violence forces me to decide who I want to be and how I want to be as a student affairs practitioner. In the short time I have been involved with the student affairs profession, I have learned to always be cautious, critical, and vigilant of how I interact with settler colonial logics and how I negotiate with them on knowledge(s), power, and culture. I will always align with my community and ancestors before anything else. My responsibility is to my community and ancestors. Yet, by placing myself in higher education, at a university far from the red mesas and juniper trees of my ancestors, my responsibility is demanded to the university. That demand caters to a possibility in which I am "entangled in resettlement, reoccupation, and reinhabitation that actually further settler colonialism" (Tuck & Yang, 2012, p. 1). The demand to almost further settler colonialism frightens me and has me questioning if I can truly be in the student affairs profession. The slightest possibility of settler colonial entanglement has me wanting to actively aspire for decolonization. Through decolonization, I can minimize the instruction of settler colonial logics through a composition of Indigenous conceptions of culture, power, and knowledge. Linda Tuhiwai Smith (2012), a Ngati Awa and Ngati Porou scholar, further posited that:

> Decolonization, however, does not mean and has not meant a total rejection of all theory or research or Western Knowledge. Rather, it is about centering our concerns and world views and then coming to know and understand theory and research from our own perspectives and for our own purposes. (p. 41)

The need to center my own concerns and worldview is crucial in understanding the daily operations and battles against settler colonialism that many Indigenous Peoples face daily and intergenerationally. The aspiration for decolonization is a matter of survival for many of us, especially as we interact closely with settler colonial logics daily. My survival hinges on the integration and internalization of Indigenous notions of culture, power, and knowledge(s), which take on new meanings that are pivotal in a decolonial engagement with education. Tribal Critical Race Theory (TribalCrit) informs these new meanings. Culture becomes conceptualized as connected to the lands on which Indigenous communities live as well as their ancestors, who lived on those lands since time immemorial (Brayboy, 2006). Indigenous Peoples "are shaped by their cultural inheritance, and they engage in cultural production" (Brayboy, 2006, p. 434) as do all human societies. Culture is what makes up life and the intimate relationship(s) that particular Indigenous communities have to the lands they live on. Indigenous notions of culture differ from what "culture" is considered in the student affairs profession. It is locally situated and intimate with those who have lived on the lands before. Decolonization requires the return of Indigenous life and land, or culture, which allows the intimate relationships that Indigenous Peoples have to reoccur.

Indigenous notions of power distract from settler colonial conceptions, the exertion of control and domination of another. It is because of this distraction that TribalCrit suggests difficulty in describing "power." Brayboy (2006) proposed themes drawn from other Indigenous scholars, for understanding what is "power" and wrote that power is not a "property or trait that an individual has to exercise control over others; rather it is rooted in a group's ability to define themselves, their place in the world, and their traditions" (p. 435). These notions of power may emerge through Indigenous communities' ability to retain and continue the existence of both their language and their stories. Having access to such mechanism of expression are crucial for a decolonial approach and understanding. Brayboy (2006) later defined "power" as the "ability to survive rooted in the capacity to adapt and adjust to changing landscapes, times, ideas, circumstances, and situations" (p. 435). The ability for Indigenous Peoples to define themselves is related to meaningful survival(s) against the onslaught of settler colonial logics. The loss or corruption of such ability correlates to a loss of Indigenous notions of "power." The lack of support or encouragement of such an ability from the student affairs profession for Indigenous youth indicates the limitations and innate colonization of higher education.

Knowledge is not singular; rather knowledge(s) vary within situations and the context of discourses. Brayboy (2006) defines knowledge(s) as the "ability to recognize change, adapt, and move forward with the change" (p. 434). Brayboy further posits that "cultural" knowledge, knowledge of survival, and "academic" knowledge are the forms of knowledges that manifest for Indigenous Peoples. Cultural knowledge is "an understanding of what it means to be a member of a particular tribal nation; this includes particular traditions, issues, and ways of being and knowing that make an individual a member of [the] community" (Brayboy, 2006, p. 434). Knowledge of survival is understanding "how and in what ways change can be accomplished and the ability and willingness to change, adapt, and adjust to move forward as an individual and community" (Brayboy, 2006, pp. 434–435). Academic knowledge is the knowledge accrued from "educational institutions," which are those within settler colonizers social systems. Knowledge is about the recognition of change, and adapting to that change while in harmony with the world and the cosmos. These varying notions of knowledge(s) are essential for the capabilities that Indigenous Peoples bring with them to higher education and more. The conceptions of culture, power, and knowledge(s) correlates with the possibility of holistic development and engagement that the student affairs profession is trying to achieve. It is only that of settler colonial logics that limits our understandings and possibilities of Indigenous capabilities. TribalCrit's outline of knowledge(s) challenged what higher education considers to be key for academic success and preparation.

In indigenized systems, culture, power, and knowledge(s) comprise the ideology of Indigenous Peoples in ways that the "we" become the subject and not the "I" because of the amalgamation, interconnection of personhoods, and communalistic aspects that comprise their identities. Culture, power, and knowledge(s) procure a relational understanding of the self and the responsibilities. All three conceptions are dialogical; Brayboy (2006) posited, "culture is the base for knowledge that ultimately leads to power" (p. 436). Through having a cultural social system, the knowledge developed within that culture allows for axes of power to become defined and refined. Yet, these relational understandings recognize and highlight the need for change, adaptation, and moving forward, implying that Indigenous ways of knowing and being(s) are fluid and dynamic in their construction and their continuation, especially in their goals of resistance and decolonization. Such a complex understanding provides the basis for decolonial engagement and development as mechanisms of navigation, resistance, and survival. The student affairs profession can begin advocating and institutionalizing such support and build upon a liberating educational system. Integrating or at least recognizing and giving reassurances to such indigenized approaches are imperative for my own decolonial engagement.

The need to create spaces for indigenized resistance and modules of decolonization requires many of us, especially within the student affairs profession, to do more, achieve more, accrue more of whatever prompts a liberating future. At the epicenter, Indigenous liberation requires Indigenous Peoples to be *hypervisible*. Brayboy (2004) writes that "visibility can lead to surveillance, marginalization, and ostracism, while simultaneously having positive consequences that are directly related to strategic forms of activism, advocacy, and the maintenance of cultural integrity" (p. 146). Indigenous Peoples are constantly under surveillance from ourselves, from our communities, and from foreign social systems. The consequences of the consciousness of our marginalization, our oppressed status, and our colonization implore us to develop strategic forms of activism, advocacy, coping mechanisms, and reclaiming knowledge denied to us. Visibility forces Indigenous Peoples "to choose between the lesser of two evils: retreating into the silence and invisibility that are more comfortable or challenging inaccurate representations and sharing information about what 'real' Indians are, and thus becoming more visible" (Brayboy, 2004, p. 146) in various social settings. Indigenous Peoples are forced to decide between remaining in the shadows and the comforts of their communities and letting the violence continue or they are asked to become *visible* and tasked with advocating, unsettling, and reminding non-Natives who they are, who they have been, and who they will be. There is a decision to be made—to either be visible or invisible. One that requires resiliency and delineation from the current settler colonial regime.

After finishing the first year of my job, I continued to be surprised seeing the flag of the Narragansett Indian Tribe. In many ways, the flag represents the decision that Indigenous Peoples are forced to make, we either choose to be invisible or we choose to be visible. In this instance, whoever placed the flag in this room, chose to be visible. In my first-year as an emerging higher education practitioner, I realized that I must consistently reframe and, in some cases, attempt to indigenize a space to be able to center and amplify Indigenous voices. I am choosing to be visible, to challenge higher education and its own settler colonial logics; but in the face of the colonial academy, I am one person. I cannot change a profession that is not willing to listen. But the field of student affairs lies, alongside many other social systems, at the edge of a precipice. It is a time of immense change as injustices happen every day. Just as it has been used to colonize, education can be an apparatus for liberation.

Indigenous students are expected to adhere to the cultural transmission and enrichment of the "United States" within higher education. This philosophy is preserved and presented in many contemporary student affairs literature with a focus on holistic student development and engagement. In the recent fourth edition of *The Handbook of Student Affairs Administration*, the field is, at its essence, focused on helping and supporting every student to get the most out of their own collegiate experiences. Student affairs strives for "changing the world for the better" (Coomes & Gerda, 2016, p. 3) and being a catalyst for lifelong transformation. The reasoning for student affairs is to help students, to "step back and view both the students and the college experience as a whole" (Coomes & Gerda, 2016, p. 4). Yet, with regards to the seminal documents and the founding of American education, it is critical to inquire who exactly is getting the most out of their own collegiate experiences. Indigenous students are being left behind in the catalyst for lifelong transformation because of their erasure and omission in student affairs literature and the statistics of education. It would be a disservice to the present student affairs philosophy to not go beyond the asterisk, the phenomenon of excluding and being "written out of the higher education story" (Shotton, Lowe, & Waterman, 2013, p. 2) based upon limited or lack of significant data for Indigenous Peoples. The field of student affairs is failing if it does not recognize and confront the deeply embedded settler colonial logics within its history and the spaces that guide and affect their work. It is an unfortunate reality that the academic systems of higher education "implicitly or explicitly try to zero out difference" (James, 2004, p. 65) to streamline their efforts of diversity and inclusion. Erasing differences and attaining a culture of sameness is a violent process, especially towards communities who already have a unique and established sense of culture, power, and knowledge(s). It is time for the profession of student affairs to decide to adhere to the current philosophy of helping and supporting *all* students in meaningful ways as has been advocated by Coomes and Gerda (2016) or continue to be a tool of colonization and violence towards Indigenous communities. It cannot be emphasized enough that the key to indigenous liberation is that of acknowledgement and building meaningful relationships with local Indigenous communities. In the coming days, weeks, and/or months, there needs to be moments where Indigenous voices are heard and affirmed without a constant reproduction of colonial attitudes or violence against us. The field of student affairs needs to interrogate and recognize the violence that is reproduced and understand how intimate the field's history is with settler colonial violence and displacement.

I, too, have a decision to make. I believe there is something salvageable about education, a possible existence in an indigenized future. Ever since the era of biological warfare from the early European-American colonizers, Indigenous Peoples have fought tooth and nail to survive and regain access to resources stolen from them. Presently, we choose to resist and challenge the dominant narratives. We choose to advocate for decolonization, demanding the return of our own lands and life. The trajectory of the world is shifting and many communities considered insignificant are reclaiming spaces stolen and/or denied to them from the colonizers. The aspiration for decolonization empowers Indigenous Peoples. Decolonization demands for the "belief and trust in our own peoples' values and abilities, and a willingness to make change" (Wilson, 2004, p. 71). Decolonial engagement is no longer about survival; rather it is about restoration and returning to our own sense of culture, power, and knowledge(s).

As an emerging student affairs practitioner, I am responsible for carving out a space outside the logics of settler colonialism. My decided visibility portrays my capability of navigating and surviving the violence of settler colonial logics. My retention of my culture and knowledge(s) provide me the basis for decolonial engagement and evidently, liberation for myself and for the communities I represent as an Indigenous person. My visibility is more than one person; it is the product of generations of inherited resilience and survivors. As written in my professional philosophy in 2017,

> I am informed by forms of consciousness, ancestral and colonialism, that I must be critical of my creation and socializations…It is my responsibility as a sacred being, endowed with the wisdom and knowledge of my ancestors, to be competent, to be empathetic, to be intentional, to be authentic, to be truthful, and to be attuned to the needs of my body, my heart, my mind, my spirit, my ancestors, my family, and my community within my various lives—as a child, as a sibling, as a guardian, as a healer, as a teacher, as a professional, as a scholar, and as a human being.

Just like the single flag of the Narragansett Indian Tribe I see at my job, I am prepared to carve out the space for my people in the field of student affairs. I am endowed with the wisdom and strength of my ancestors, both healers and warriors, who encourage, and even urge me, to be visible. My decision has been made and I will survive. Settler colonial logics have nothing on the origins of my communities' culture, power, and knowledge(s). I am ready, but is the field ready?

REFERENCES

Althusser, L. (1971). Ideology and ideological state apparatuses (notes towards an investigation). In *Lenin and philosophy and other essays* (Translated from the French by Ben Brewster [pp. 127–186]). New York, NY: Monthly Review Press.

American Council on Education. (1937). *The student personnel point of view: A report of a conference on the philosophy and development of student personnel work in college and university* (Series 1, Vol. 1, No. 3). Washington, DC: Author.

American Council on Education. (1949). *The student personnel point of view* (Rev. ed., Series 6, No. 13). Washington, DC: Author.

Arvin, M., Tuck, E., & Morrill, A. (2013). Decolonizing feminism: Challenging connections between settler colonialism and heteropatriarchy. *Feminist Formations*, *25*(1), 8–34. Retrieved from http://www.jstor.org/stable/43860665

Brayboy, B. M. (2004). Hiding in the ivy: American Indian students and visibility in elite educational settings. *Harvard Educational Review*, *74*(2), 125–152. doi:10.17763/haer.74.2.x141415v38360mg4

Brayboy, B. M. (2006). Toward a tribal critical race theory in education. *The Urban Review*, *37*(5), 425–446. doi:10.1007/s11256-005-0018-y

Brayboy, B. M., Fann, A. J., Castagno, A. E., & Solyom, J. A. (2012). Postsecondary education for American Indian and Alaska Natives: Higher education for nation building and self-determination. *ASHE Higher Education Report*, *37*(5).

Coomes, M. D., & Gerda, J. J. (2016). A long and honorable history: Student affairs in the United States. In G. McClellan & J., &. Stringer (Eds.), *The handbook of student affairs administration* (4th ed., pp. 3–23). San Francisco, CA: Jossey-Bass.

James, K. (2004). Corrupt state university: The organizational psychology of Native experience in higher education. In D. A. Mihesuah & A. C. Wilson (Eds.), *Indigenizing the academy: Transforming scholarship and empowering communities* (pp. 48–68). Lincoln: University of Nebraska Press.

Okihiro, G. Y. (2016). *Third world studies: Theorizing liberation*. Durham, NC: Duke University Press Books.

Shotton, H. J., Lowe, S. C., & Waterman, S. J. (Eds.). (2013). *Beyond the asterisk: Understanding Native students in higher education*. Sterling, VA: Stylus.

Smith, L. T. (2012). *Decolonizing methodologies: Research and Indigenous Peoples*. London, England: Zed Books.

Tuck, E., & Yang, K. (2012). Decolonization is not a metaphor. *Decolonization: Indigeneity, Education, & Society*, *1*(1), 1–40. Retrieved from https://jps.library.utoronto.ca/index.php/des/article/view/18630

Wilson, A. C. (2004). Reclaiming our humanity: Decolonization and the recovery of Indigenous knowledge. In D. A. Mihesuah & A. C. Wilson (Eds.), *Indigenizing the academy: Transforming scholarship and empowering communities* (pp. 69–87). Lincoln: University of Nebraska Press.

CHAPTER 15

CONFESSIONS OF A FIRST-YEAR PROFESSIONAL

Thaddeus R. Stegall
New York University Abu Dhabi

The experiences of a first-year student affairs professional of color is examined to shed light on the challenges faced in the first year of professional practice and the tools and strategies used to overcome them. Throughout the first year, the author had the opportunity to reflect on his experience and how to improve his performance through professional development. This chapter explores the journey through the lenses of self-awareness, critical reflection, and radical self-love.

With a substantial population of the profession being new professionals—first time, full-time professionals with five or fewer years of experience—it is imperative to explore their experience, growth, and development. A sense of urgency exists to explore the challenges and needs of new professionals due to the alarming rate of attrition in student affairs and higher education. While the exact percentage of new professionals that leave the field within the first five years is debatable (Lorden, 1998), scholars (Renn & Jessup-Anger, 2008) have cited the level of attrition ranging between 50%–60%.

No Ways Tired, pages 129–139

Many scholars (Lorden, 1998; Renn & Jessup-Anger, 2008; Tull, 2006) cite job satisfaction, or lack thereof, as the main culprit for the high attrition rate amongst new professionals. Prevalent factors contributing to job dissatisfaction include role ambiguity, lack of supervisory or institutional support, job burnout, and the despondency of career mobility (Lorden, 1998; Renn & Jessup-Anger, 2008; Tull, 2006). Renn and Jessup-Anger (2009) offer sound solutions to address attrition including improving the supervision and professional development of new professionals. Cilente, Henning, Skinner Jackson, Kennedy, and Sloan (2006) assert the three most pressing professional development needs amongst new professionals are receiving adequate support, understanding job expectations, and fostering student learning. These needs present a significant challenge to new professionals and their growth, development, and career longevity.

Ardoin (2014) believes professional development is "your responsibility. Instead of professional development, the term should really be self-development in your profession, because that is where the responsibilities lie" (p. 89). The three aforementioned areas of professional development will be discussed through the lenses of self-awareness, critical reflection, and radical self-love and explained through the #FirstYearConfessions social media campaign facilitated by the author during his first year in the profession. The #FirstYearConfessions campaign sheds light on two key takeaways: you are the only person you can change and your time, energy, and talent are your most precious resources.

SELF-AWARENESS

Self-awareness is critical to professional development. ACPA and NASPA (2015) have done extensive work to provide student affairs professionals with outcome-based competencies to guide their personal and professional development. The personal and ethical foundations (PEF) competency serves as a rubric involving,

> the knowledge, skills, and dispositions to develop and maintain integrity in one's life and work; this [the development of integrity] includes thoughtful development, critique, and adherence to a holistic and comprehensive standard of ethics and commitment to one's own wellness and growth. (p. 16)

Specifically, a "commitment to one's own wellness and growth" (ACPA & NASPA, 2015, p. 16) requires professionals to have awareness of self and awareness/knowledge of their relationships with others. The most important relationships to be aware of are those with colleagues, supervisees, superiors, and students. Self-awareness is important as it influences the professional of color's perception of their relationships with others at the institution.

ACPA and NASPA (2015) challenge professionals to "articulate awareness and understanding of one's attitudes, values, beliefs, assumptions, biases, and identify how they affect one's integrity and work with others" (p. 16). The previously mentioned outcome is listed as foundational and is relevant to the development of new/entry-level student affairs professionals. A professional's attitude, assumptions, and biases impact how they view their work and what is expected of them. Self-awareness provided me with an internal compass to understand my purpose and definition of success, especially as a professional of color. While my journey towards self-awareness began well before entering my graduate program, I received a much needed self-awareness check my first year in graduate school.

As a social justice advocate, I thought too highly of myself on the proverbial scale of sleep to woke. I recall scrolling through twitter and seeing the tweet, "If you are pro Black but anti-gay you don't want equality you want privilege" (JUSLIKEMIKE863, 2015). I remember experiencing a state of shock triggered by the incongruence between who I thought I was and who this tweet suggested I might be. I lacked self-awareness because my behavior did not align with my values. My journey towards self-awareness began with critical reflection. Critical reflection, a thoughtful critique of my values and beliefs (Mezirow, 1990), led me to the importance of listening to my inner voice, regardless of what it was saying. Accepting my inner voice led me to a more intimate and nuanced self-awareness. My ever-progressing self-awareness guided me towards congruence between my values and behavior.

UNDERSTANDING JOB EXPECTATIONS

It ain't always about being right, it's about getting it right.
—Antonio L. Pee #SAPro #FirstYearConfessions #HigherEducation

One of my heart's desires is to be right; the authority on all things correct, moral, and socially just, including the truth—"A superlative. The greatest or most positive form it is possible for a person or thing to be" (Ca$hmir, 2003). At times, my desire to be the truth impeded the fulfillment of my job expectations—including supervision, administration, paraprofessional counseling, community development, and institutional collaboration. I was expected to fulfill my job duties ethically, efficiently, and effectively. My ego often took a front seat and impaired my ability to listen with empathy, lead collaboratively, and take a developmental approach to supervision. My efficiency and effectiveness were often challenged when dealing with difficult students. I found myself feeding the desire to be right and imposing my ideas on students. After reflecting and speaking to a mentor, I realized my priority should be getting it right.

Getting it right placed the priority on the group product and not my individual input. Getting it right challenged me to "take responsibility to broaden perspectives by participating in activities that challenged my beliefs" (ACPA & NASPA, 2015, p. 16). Getting it right challenged me to be part of something bigger than me and contribute to its success.

FOSTERING STUDENT LEARNING

One of the harshest realizations as a first-year #SAPro is that everyone doesn't want to be developed.

#FirstYearConfessions

You can't be everything to everyone.

#SAPro #FirstYearConfessions #HigherEducation

In graduate school I learned the importance of student development and support. I accepted that *in loco parentis*—in place of parents—was my professional charge, purpose, and mission. Student development was my theory, my practice, and justification for my existence as a professional. I existed to provide students with what they needed to be successful adults, including a balance of challenge and support. I was rendered ineffective when one of my resident assistants (RAs) began to rebel against the development I aimed to provide. Their disdain for development was difficult for me to process as the crux of my responsibility to them, from my perspective, was their development. I processed everything that took place and realized the need to reflect and become aware of the "attitudes, values, beliefs, assumptions, [and] biases" (ACPA & NASPA, 2015, p. 16) that impacted my work with students. While the student remained resistant in my attempts for support, they did seek support from one of my closest colleagues. Toward the end of the year, my strategy was to get the student to the finish line, at all costs. I believed my responsibility was to develop everyone. This perceived responsibility amplified the amount of disappointment I felt when I realized everyone doesn't want to be developed.

As a student affairs professional of color, we are overwhelmingly socialized to believe we should be in-service to everyone, sometimes even at the cost of our well-being. Our collective history highlights notions of marginalization and second-class citizenry that relegate people of color to service-oriented callings. I realized the responsibility to develop everyone was not held in the same regard by many, but not all, of my colleagues who were not people of color. My belief in the omniscient power of seminal student development theories often left out the lived experiences of the marginalized student and the international student. As a professional of color, I was empathetic to their struggle of marginalization and felt obligated to connect with them to provide additional support. This shared connection produced authentic conversations laced with terms of endearment and code switching. These authentic conversations often garnered unwelcomed and microaggressive glares from colleagues. This experience taught me that everyone doesn't want to be developed, and their development is not my job alone.

CRITICAL REFLECTION

Reflection is essential to self-awareness and engaging in radical self-love. ACPA and NASPA (2015) call professionals to "recognize the importance of reflection in personal, professional, and ethical development" (p. 16). In order to reflect, one must make meaning. Making meaning involves defining, interpreting, making sense, and subscribing value to an experience (Mezirow, 1990). Meaning turns into learning when the value of an experience is used to guide decision-making (Mezirow, 1990). Learning through reflection assists professionals in understanding job expectations and fostering student learning.

Reflection requires one to make meaning, while critical reflection involves a focus on growth instead of results. This focus fosters a deeper commitment to the process, regardless of the outcome. Critical reflection demands great perseverance as it "involves a critique of the presuppositions on which our beliefs have been built" (Mezirow, 1990, p. 1). It demands that one takes a deep dive into themselves to find both the characteristics that are great and the aspects that need to be improved.

During my first year, my values were challenged consistently. Students often advocated for things like priority housing registration and exceptions to policies, procedures, and accountability. The students' desires for privilege caused conflict between my values of student activism and social justice. Through critical reflection, I realized that social justice was more important to me than was student activism. My affinity towards social justice over student activism, in this instance, reflected and honored the many sacrifices people of color have made and continue to make to be present in educational and professional spaces around the world. My newly aligned values compelled me to challenge students to think critically about the things they were advocating for and how their desires impeded upon the rights and opportunities of others. As a professional of color who values social justice over student activism, it is my responsibility to create and advocate for systems and structures that are sustainable, efficient, and equitable for all students, while valuing the student voice and perspective.

UNDERSTANDING JOB EXPECTATIONS

How would you make decisions if you knew that each one would become precedent?
Always remember, quick fixes become precedent, precedent becomes tradition,
and we all know tradition is law, or do we?

#SAPro #FirstYearConfessions #HigherEducation

Decision-making was one of the most persistent challenges of my first year. While working at a young institution provided me with the invigorating opportunity to create, my innovation required wisdom. Wisdom, in this context, was institutional knowledge applied with a wide-angle lens to understand its impact on the intelligent, over-engaged, international, and privileged student body. Wisdom required me to understand "the professional culture here is centered on the care of the individual student" (Hirt, 2006, p. 27). The successful relationships I built with students taught me they want to be treated as individuals, yet their standard for acceptable treatment was defined by how I treated their peers.

Equipped with knowledge and wisdom, I was better prepared to be innovative and decisive. The most powerful part of this process was the level of criticality with which I began to make decisions. Before making a decision, I weighed the individual and collective student response, operational ramifications, and personal and professional ethics. As a person of color, the considerations enabled me, to the best of my ability, to make decisions that would stand the test of time and student scrutiny.

FOSTERING STUDENT LEARNING

Process vs. Product. The product may not always be transferable but the skills learned
during the process always will be.

#Evaluations #SAPro #FirstYearConfessions #HigherEducation

Process versus product challenges professionals to choose which aspect of learning is more important—the results or the journey leading to the results. While results indicate that a student has mastered a skill or task, the journey prepares the student to understand how and why they arrived at said result(s). A singular focus on the product facilitates a transactional experience and may motivate the learner to find shortcuts instead of thinking critically. Fostering student learning in this way is counter-productive to holistic student development. A focus on the process acknowledges the inquiry-based nature of knowledge production and commits to critical reflection and growth.

Process-minded knowledge production is student-centered learning that invites the student to take an active role in the experience. The invitation extended to students in process-minded knowledge production is transformative and skill building. Through this transformative learning experience, students learn and exercise critical thinking, intellectual flexibility, and perseverance. Transformative learning occurs when students "encounter an alternative perspective and prior habits of mind are called into question" (Cranton, 2006, p. 23). To resolve tension produced by an alternative perspective and prior habits of mind, students reflect on the process and ask critical questions such as: "How did this come to be" (Cranton, 2006, p. 34). Resolving this inner conflict places a spotlight on the process and the importance of critical reflection.

Throughout my first year in the profession, students often entrusted me with their issues, challenges, and concerns. As a professional who values process over product, I wanted our students to grow from the experience of working alongside professionals to find a solution to the challenges they faced, instead of implementing a reactive solution.

RADICAL SELF-LOVE

ACPA and NASPA (2015) invite student affairs professionals to "bolster [their] resiliency, including participating in stress-management activities, engaging in personal or spiritual exploration, and building healthier relationships inside and outside of the workplace" (p. 17). This outcome highlights the importance of personal health and well-being. The beginning of a healthy personal life is an attentive focus on self that requires some, but not all encapsulating, selfishness. Selfishness—"characterized by or manifesting concern or care only for oneself" (Selfish, n.d.)—"is a significant dimension of true self-love" (Lippitt, 2009, p. 136). Excellence in self-care is too often overlooked because of the moral implications that commonly accompany selfishness (Lippitt, 2009). Perfecting the art of taking care of yourself can imply a lack of regard for the needs of others and the impact you may have on them. While selfishness is often looked down upon, it is deemed unacceptable for people of color. Because of our history of collective struggle, people of color are expected to be docile, selfless, and willing to freely give of their time, energy, and talent. Any narrative counter to this social construction of Blackness calls in to question one's morality and proximity to Blackness.

My first year in the profession taught me the importance of radical self-love. I often found myself physically exhausted and emotionally drained. At first, I blamed my environment for the early onset of burnout. After critical reflection, I realized my health and well-being were my prerogative and they needed to become my priority. The most important way I began to exercise self-care was to leave the office on time. Leaving at the end of the workday was a safeguard for the time, energy, and talent that is often seen as endless for people of color. Secondly, I was adamant about #ReclaimingMyTime by not responding to text messages, emails, and phone calls on the weekends (while not on-call). Next, I used my free time to engage in stress-relieving activities catered to my interests such as intramural sports and hosting a radio show on the student-run radio station. I also spent time outside of work cultivating friendships and new hobbies, learning about the region I had just moved to, and spending mass amounts of time on FaceTime with my partner and family, all of whom were on another continent.

RECEIVING ADEQUATE SUPPORT

You cannot wait for the intuition to validate your work.

At times throughout my first year, I struggled due to a lack support and validation. There were times I felt alone or that my excitement and inno-vation were neither welcomed nor appreciated. I struggled to accept that my students did not want to be developed, which is the difficult side of our work that new professionals seldom talk about. While in this sunken place, I began to reflect on my experience and think critically about how to move forward.

After fruitful conversations with mentors, I realized I could not wait for the institution or anyone else to validate my work. I was validated because I made a conscious effort to love myself fearlessly—the good, the bad, and the ugly. I found peace by "participating in stress-management activities, engaging in personal or spiritual exploration, and building healthier re-lationships inside and outside of the workplace" (ACPA & NASPA, 2015, p. 17). I chose to love myself by focusing on my relationships, playing intra-mural basketball, and writing again.

CONCLUSION

While my professional journey is just beginning, I acknowledge the impor-tance of self-awareness, critical reflection, and radical self-love. My first year in the profession taught me to be aware of myself and the impact of that awareness on those around me. I learned it is critical to reflect often. Critical reflection helped me fall in love with the difficult process of bettering myself. My first year taught me that I am enough. I cannot let my job or my career define how I feel about myself. My mental, physical, and spiritual health are intimately connected and are more important than my career. If I am not ok and healthy, I cannot help anyone else be okay. Succinctly put, my first year taught me the importance of my time, my energy, and my talent.

RECOMMENDATIONS

I have provided two key takeaways for new professionals of color. I hope the takeaways will aid professionals in making informed decisions about their career, values, and personal and professional development.

"God grant me the serenity to accept the people I cannot change, the courage to change the one I can, and the wisdom to know-it's me!" (Miller, 2004). #Message #SAPro #FirstYearConfessions

Firstly, you are the only person you can change and the Serenity Prayer is a great reminder. The Serenity Prayer, attributed to Reinhold Niebuhr in 1933, has been coined as the most famous and beloved prayer of the 20th century (Shapiro, 2014). The prayer is commonly recited, "God grant me the serenity to accept the things I cannot change, courage to change the things I can, and wisdom to know the difference" (Shapiro, 2014, para. 1). The quote from *Question Behind the Question* (2004) is an adaptation of the Serenity Prayer that speaks to the power of personal accountability. The book was a gift from my cousin, Rod Williams, an award-winning realtor in Atlanta, Georgia, who gives me books for personal and professional growth every year. The quote empowered me to re-evaluate my performance. Specifically, it challenged me to examine the immense amount of power I had over myself and the outcomes I experienced.

While I do not have the power to change the outcome of many situations I face, I have the power to alter my disposition and choose my reaction, even if that reaction is indifference. Wisdom is knowledge, actualized appropriately with discernment and insight (Wisdom, n.d.). Wisdom required me to have knowledge with a lens wide enough to understand the peripheral ramifications of its use. Having the wisdom to know I was the only person I could change, necessitated a knowledge of self, knowledge of the impact I had on others, and a knowledge of the systems that I lived and worked in. While this newfound knowledge did not change my job expectations, it did change my disposition toward them. This approach made excellence the norm and consistency the goal. When excellence and consistency became the norm by which I evaluated my personal accountability, my work with students became less taxing, more transformational, and more rewarding.

Everyone and everything don't deserve your time, energy, and talent. Be sure to invest them wisely. #LessonLearned #SAPro #FirstYearConfessions #HigherEducation

Love yourself fully. Many people of color and people with other marginalized identities don't have the privilege to authentically bring all of who they are to work each day. Showing up in a space that doesn't acknowledge, accept, tolerate, or welcome all of you can be incredibly taxing and demoralizing. Serving students in places that don't deserve your time, energy, and talent can make working in student affairs an endless labor of love. This labor is full of long nights and weekends with frequent invasions into personal life. Student affairs can be incredibly unkind at times and if you fail to make yourself a priority, you can fall victim to the inequitable systems you are working to save your students from. Lastly, define, crystallize, and live by your values. Your values are your compass and non-negotiables. They should be clear, communicable, and evident in your work and your interactions with others. Your values should shape how you invest your time, energy, and talent. They should guide you in moments of ambiguity and comfort you in moments of strife. Your values should guide your decision-making, determine where you work, and define your legacy.

REFERENCES

ACPA & NASPA. (2015). *ACPA/NASPA professional competency areas for student affairs educators.* Washington, DC: Authors.

Ardoin, S. (2014). *The strategic guide to shaping your student affairs career.* Sterling, VA: Stylus.

Ca$hmir, M. (2003). The truth. In *Urban Dictionary.* Retrieved from https://www.urbandictionary.com/define.php?term=the+truth

Cilente, K., Henning, G., Skinner Jackson, J., Kennedy, D., & Sloan, T. (2006). *Report on the new professional needs study.* Washington, DC: American College Personnel Association.

Cranton, P. (2006). *Understanding and promoting transformative learning: A guide for educators of adults.* San Francisco, CA: Jossey-Bass.

Hirt, J. (2006). *Where you work matters: Student affairs administration at different types of institutions.* Lanham, MD: University Press of America, Inc.

JUSLIKEMIKE863. (2015, November 19). If you are pro Black but anti-gay you don't want equality you want privilege [Twitter Post]. Retrieved from https://twitter.com/juslikemike863/status/667215882939142146?lang=en

Lippitt, J. (2009). True self-love and true self-sacrifice. *International Journal for Philosophy of Religion, 66(3),* 125–138.

Lorden, L. P. (1998). Attrition in the student affairs profession. *NASPA Journal, 35,* 207–216.

Mezirow, J. (1990). How critical reflection triggers transformative learning. In J. Mezirow & Associates (Eds.), *Fostering critical reflection in adulthood: A guide to transformative and emancipatory learning* (pp. 1–20). San Francisco, CA: Jossey-Bass.

Miller, J. (2004). *The question behind the question: Practicing personal accountability at work and in life.* New York, NY: Penguin Random House LLC.

Renn, K. A., & Jessup-Anger, E. R. (2008). Preparing new professionals: Lessons for graduate preparation programs from the national study of new professionals in student affairs. *Journal of College Student Development, 49(4),* 319–335.

Selfish. (n.d.). In *Dictionary.com Unabridged.* Retrieved from http://www.dictionary .com/browse/selfishness

Shapiro, F. (2014, April 28). Who wrote the serenity prayer? *The Chronicle of Higher Education.* Retrieved from https://www.chronicle.com/article/Who -Wrote-the-SerenityPrayer-/146159

Tull, A. (2006). Synergistic supervision, job satisfaction, and intention to turnover of new professionals in student affairs. *Journal of College Student Development, 47,* 465–477.

Wisdom. (n.d.). In *Dictionary.com Unabridged.* Retrieved from http://www.dictionary .com/browse/wisdom

CHAPTER 16

TIRED, BUT NOT WEARY

Kevin L. Wright
University of Nevada, Las Vegas

The goal of this chapter is to shed light on the experience of navigating through the field of student affairs and higher education as a new professional with a double consciousness lens. W. E. B. Du Bois (1903) coined the term *double consciousness* as a concept to describe an individual who views specific aspects of their identity divided into several facets. This chapter will provide a forward-thinking framework to navigate towards inclusive and equitable workplace success and words of wisdom given to me by current Black administrators working in higher education.

I wake up every morning and check the news just to make sure I still have my rights. As a new professional working in student affairs and higher education, it is imperative to understand and acknowledge how the climate of the broader community affects the climate of the campus community. Furthermore, it is imperative for me to understand how I am perceived by my peers when serving my students. There are people who view me as a Black professional and there are those who view me as a professional who is Black. Until I entered this field as a graduate student, I did not think there was truly a difference. However, my way of thinking shifted when I was introduced to the concept of double consciousness. W. E. B. Du Bois authored *The Souls of Black Folk* in 1903, in which he defines double consciousness as "this sense of always looking at one's self through the eyes of others" (p. 7). Du Bois' work was published over 100 years ago, and yet, through my lived experiences, double consciousness is a relevant and timely concept in the present day. As a new professional, I operate with having to be three steps ahead of a person's assumptions about me.

EXPERIENCES AS A NEW PROFESSIONAL

As a Black man working in student affairs and higher education, a White colleague told me explicitly that I am perceived as a threat because of my diligence and empowering work ethic. Unfortunately, I have also been arrested by campus police for being perceived as someone who looked suspicious walking around campus; I was the Hall Director on duty at that time. Additionally, others tried to pigeonhole my skills and abilities toward multicultural affairs work. Yet, I continue to broaden my skills in various functional areas to obtain a breadth and depth of experiences. As a person of color working in higher education, I have been perceived as a progressive advocate for students from historically marginalized identities. I have been told the work I do with other professionals of color, who do not look like me, makes others proud to call me their colleague. As a person of color in higher education, I have had my personal experiences painted with others as if all professionals of color are a monolith, which concluded with others calling it a "mosaic of resiliency."

When my Blackness is apparent, trouble and struggle are near, but when my Blackness is not acknowledged, recognition and praise are soon to follow. Du Bois (1903) stated that double consciousness "is a peculiar sensation" and that "this sense of always looking at one's self through the eyes of others, of measuring one's soul by the tape of a world that looks on in amused contempt and pity" (p. 3). It was how he had to operate. I find myself using parts of his literature to guide how I operate as a scholar-practitioner. Specifically, the hope is to create a perception that expresses how one professional of color can work with other professionals of color and not have their racial/ethnic identity be unacknowledged by their White colleagues through the work they're doing to advance the students they serve.

In this work of inclusion, advocacy, and social justice, we cannot let our melanin be our melancholy. I have been blessed with much success and have faced much struggle at the same time. We cannot be afraid of the struggle, but rather focus on how we conduct ourselves in the struggle while we serve our students. As a new professional, there have already been times where my struggles were not acknowledged or seen. I have shown up in the workplace as Ralph Ellison (1952) describes when he says "I am an invisible man . . . I am a man of substance, of flesh and bone, fiber and liquids—and I might even be said to possess a mind. I am invisible, understand, simply because people refuse to see me" (p. 3). Enduring multiple struggles while doing the work of serving our students is exhausting. However, even though I am tired, I am not weary. Before professionals of color can move forward, we must first know where we currently are.

FORWARD FRAMEWORK

A framework new professionals can use emphasizes on the notion of collaborative advocacy and revolves around positive psychology, established to promote the best in people and institutions (Mather, 2010). Collaborative advocacy is used to encourage a conscious effort between new professionals and senior level administrators. New professionals come into the field with a sense of what they want to change about the field and are usually met with resistance because of their new status. Specifically, new professionals of color come into the field with how they can create more access for the historically marginalized. However, institutional, divisional, and departmental context helps develop their approach to creating more access. Much of this context comes from senior level administrators. By having a paradigm shift, new professionals and senior level administrators can escape from the mindset of one side versus the other (Dalton, Thompson, & Price, 1997).

Professionals of color experience microaggressions, racial stereotyping, and workplace othering, all of which undermine their achievements and sense of belonging, like experiences of students of color (Harper, 2012). For institutions that want to make more of a conscious effort to not have the work of their professionals of color unseen, engaging their strengths is required. By engaging their strengths, an opportunity is created to foster workplace success. As much as student affairs and higher education promotes and encourages scholars and practitioners to engage in a specific way to contribute to the success of our students, the field should be doing the same with its employees. We need to practice what we preach in every aspect of our role in this work. Clifton, Anderson, and Schreiner (2006) argue, "disillusionment, discouragement, and reduced motivation are more likely causes of academic failure than a lack of ability" (p. xii). The same can be said in regards to full-time professionals, especially new professionals of color.

In regards to positive psychology, it is a two-way street. New professionals tend to have perspective on how the field should look, but fail to acknowledge what the field currently is. The sense of disillusionment and disenchantment creates false perceptions of the field among new professionals, and eventually trickles into the narrative of how 50%–60% of professionals leave the field of higher education within 5 years (Lorden, 1998; Tull, 2006). While fostering a culture of inclusive and equitable initiatives, administrators need to communicate realistic expectations of their institution and its varying functional areas. Lastly, new professionals of color need to be mindful of how they navigate certain spaces while holding their personal and professional development as a top priority.

WORDS OF WISDOM

As the old African proverb states, "It takes a village to raise a child." My village in student affairs has filled me with so much wisdom and guidance; I would be remiss to not share some of those wise words with you all.

> Do what you can to not get buried in the org chart. (Dean of Students)

As a new professional, you are just getting started; be proud of where you are. Many professionals of color are aspiring to serve as senior-level administrative officers. As previous scholars (Chang, 2005; Wolfe & Freeman Jr., 2013) have indicated, the underrepresentation of administrators of color in higher education is an important ethical dilemma facing institutions in the present day. Professionals of color are needed everywhere and the value of our work is not dependent on the title on our business cards. As long as institutions are investing more on recruiting and retaining faculty and staff of color, an opportunity exists to further benefit and support our students of color. The time for being stretched too thin and experiencing workplace tokenism is up.

> Do not be a slave to another's thoughts. (Assistant Vice Chancellor)

Double consciousness can be used as a tool or a crutch for professionals of color. By using double consciousness as a tool, professionals of color develop ways to finesse through various spaces as they navigate up the ladder of the administrative hierarchy. By using double consciousness as a crutch, a professional of color is at risk of being a slave to another person's thoughts. It is okay to acknowledge and even address how one may perceive us, but their perceptions of us is not our reality; another's perception does not govern how we function or operate.

> Do not let your success be a foreign concept in the workplace. (Vice President of Student Affairs)

In the workplace, you may encounter interactions with colleagues where your success may be a surprise. Develop the habit where your accomplishments and success are expected and respected. Be strategic with your time, effort, and energy; it is not the time to be the overly involved new professional and reach burnout before the end of a semester. As new professionals of color, we need to create additional opportunities for the rising professionals coming after us. Through collaborative and restorative initiatives, professionals of color have an opportunity to further advance each other. We cannot forget why we are in student affairs to begin with. Our job is not our primary purpose in life. Our job is the vehicle that can guide us to understand our primary purpose in life. As we thrive in our jobs, we must remember our success is due to the labor of us individually and is a reflection of our community collectively.

My hope is that these words can help everyone develop additional clarity to understand their role in this work. As new professionals of color, we cannot afford to entertain or enable divisiveness. As a Black professional, I have the utmost pride in my culture and I express who I am without hesitance and yet, that behavior can still divide and separate others within the Black community or we "other" individuals in the broader people of color community. Professionals of color are already aware of what their White counterparts are doing to divide them, but we need to acknowledge what we are doing to each other as well. We need to be willing to have the conversation and do the work to uplift and empower one another. There is no point in contributing to our own marginalization while others who do not look like us benefit from it.

DISCUSSION

Many factors affect the retention of people of color including working excessive hours, burnout, non-competitive salaries, attractive career alternatives, and loss of passion (Marshall, Gardner, Hughes, & Lowery, 2016). Furthermore, institutions need to create spaces to explore the following questions:

- How does the underrepresentation of professionals of color in the workplace impact our campus community?
- Who else needs to be a part of the conversation about retaining professionals of color other than people of color?
- How can professionals of color further contribute to collective advancement and alleviate horizontal oppression within the workplace?
- How can allies and advocates contribute to dismantling a culture where workplace resiliency is a requirement and necessity for professionals of color?
- How can current scholars and practitioners create a new approach to professional success that is inclusive to all professionals of color?

The discussion about retaining professionals of color does not end with this chapter or this book. Additional dialogue at institutions amongst the decision makers is crucial. The success of professionals of color cannot go unacknowledged. With all the accolades professionals of color are achieving, we must not forget we are doing this to create space for those who do not have voice or opportunity to advance without the work we are currently producing.

CONCLUSION

Double consciousness is not solely cognitive. Initially, double consciousness was simply the way one thinks about themselves and compares it to how they think the world views them within a dichotomous mindset. As time progressed and intersectionality of identity became a concept of extensive thought and conversation, double consciousness evolved. Currently, a professional of color must have the capacity to critically analyze how they view their salient and non-salient identities, and potentially, balance it with how their White counterparts perceive them while evaluating which of their identities is being judged more than the other. I am aware of my salient identity of being Black, and yet, it is crucial for me to be mindful of my Christian values, heteronormative ideologies, and how my masculinity may inform or determine the experiences I have in certain spaces. Double consciousness was once, figuratively and literally, a Black and White concept, but now it has gotten more complicated. The current sense of complex consciousness is exhausting for professionals of color to hold. In the workplace, the value of our work needs to be evaluated by the quality of the work itself, not by the traits of our identity. The alleviation of a professional of color constantly looking at themselves through the eyes of others requires continuous dialogue, explicit acknowledgement of bias, and initiatives designed to retain, develop, and advance them. The workplace is meant for opportunity, not oppression.

REFERENCES

Chang, M. (2005). Reconsidering the diversity rationale. *Liberal Education, 91*(1), 6–13.

Clifton, D. O., Anderson, E., & Schreiner, L. A. (2006). *StrengthsQuest: Discover and develop your strengths in academics, career, and beyond* (2nd ed.). New York, NY: Gallup Press.

Dalton, G. W., Thompson, P. H., & Price, R. L. (1977). The four stages of professional careers—A new look at performance by professionals. *Organizational Dynamics, 6*(1), 19–42. https://doi.org/10.1016/0090-2616(77)90033-X

Du Bois, W. E. B. (1903). *The souls of Black folk.* New York, NY: Random House.

Ellison, R. (1952). *Invisible man.* New York, NY: Vintage International.

Harper, S. R. (2012). *Black male student success in higher education: A report from the national Black male college achievement study.* Philadelphia: University of Pennsylvania, Center for the Study of Race and Equity in Education.

Lorden, L. (1998). Attrition in the student affairs profession. *NASPA Journal, 35*(3), 207–216.

Marshall, S. M., Gardner, M. M., Hughes, C., & Lowery, U. (2016). Attrition from student affairs: Perspectives from those who exited the profession. *Journal of Student Affairs Research and Practice, 53*(2), 146–159.

Mather, P. C. (2010). Positive psychology and student affairs practice: A framework of Possibility. *Journal of Student Affairs Research and Practice, 47*(2), 157–173.

Tull, A. (2006). Synergistic supervision, job satisfaction, and intention to turn over of new professionals in student affairs. *Journal of College Student Development, 47*(4), 465–480.

Wolfe, B., & Freeman Jr, S. (2013). A case for administrators of color: Insights and policy implications for higher education's predominantly White institutions. *eJEP: eJournal of Education Policy.* Retrieved from https://files.eric.ed.gov/fulltext/EJ1158580.pdf

CONCLUDING THOUGHTS

Lift Every Voice and Sing

Monica Galloway Burke and U. Monique Robinson

The collective voice formed by the narratives in the book is enlightening and powerful. The authors were open and reflective in sharing their experiences and we are sure that some of the shared experiences will resonate with many professionals of color in student affairs. Often, we both found ourselves nodding our heads, saying "Amen," and feeling the emotion and genuineness emanating from their words. Our hope is that anyone who reads their narratives will respect their journey, recognize their tenacity, and feel uplifted.

By cultivating a collective voice, seeds can be planted to sprout awareness and hopefully, those who become aware will then cultivate an environment that truly reflects the diversity, inclusion, and respect that higher education institutions espouse in their mission and vision statements. It is human nature for an individual to desire feeling welcomed and appreciated for their efforts and every human deserves to feel safe in their space. However, as detailed in the narratives, those spaces for professionals of color can be filled with censure, discrimination, bias, stereotypes, filtered expectations, insults, passive aggressiveness, confusion, isolation, disrespect, tokenism, manipulation, and cultural blindness. Fortunately, such unpleasant

No Ways Tired, pages 149–153
Copyright © 2019 by Information Age Publishing
All rights of reproduction in any form reserved.

experiences can be tempered or countered through support, knowledge, and development.

The browning of America precipitates the need for more student affairs professionals of color at all levels at colleges and universities. The very presence of professionals of color enhances the lives of students, particularly students of color, and the overall campus climate. Their lived experiences are valid and real and acknowledgement of these experiences by staff of color makes students feel supported and heard.

No Ways Tired endeavors to give voice to the often-marginalized student affairs professionals of color, allowing them the space to be their authentic selves. We spend much of our time pouring into others and giving back and subsequently, as these narratives indicate, self-awareness, self-care, and self-preservation become a critical part of our journey. We must take care of ourselves and each other so the important work we do is sustainable, credible, ever evolving, and relevant.

Insights from the narratives also provide practical strategies to potentially enhance the endurance and career mobility of professionals of color in student affairs. Professionals of color in student affairs should use strategies to develop professionally, engage in self-care, as well as sustain and protect themselves. In addition, they should use reflective analysis and their personal *board of directors*' counsel to recognize when it is time to move on to pursue other opportunities to enhance their professional lives when the situation is emotional harmful. Taking such chances involves intentional efforts to enhance professional growth and marketability and create social capital.

Salient themes for the professionals of color emerged from the narratives as well as perceptible strategies. The themes included:

- Dealing with difficult societal structures such as the "Black Tax—an axiom that refers to how Black people must work harder than their White counterparts to achieve similar outcome; the model minority myth—the view that Asian American and Pacific Islanders are a monolithically hardworking racial group whose high achievement undercuts claims of systemic racism made by other racially minoritized populations within the institutional contexts and double burden—the multifaceted disparities experienced because of the duality of race and their gender.
- Racial and ethnic identity (e.g., Indigenous, African American, Black, Biracial, Multiracial, Latinx, Chicano, and Nigerian American) and gender/sexual identity being linked to the professional identity of professionals of color.
- Self-confidence and self-efficacy being eroded and infiltrated by imposter syndrome and double consciousness.

- Commonly being subjected to the personal responsibility and professional expectation from colleagues to consistently support students of color (e.g., other mothering) and serve as the "diversity guru" when needed, whether in our job description or not.
- Facing and surviving microaggressions and macroaggressions as well as racial battle fatigue while trying to survive and thrive in their personal and professional lives.
- The absence of meritocracy for professionals of color when it comes to opportunities and promotions.
- Marginalization and isolation, which can manifest through subtle or overt actions, impacting the social, emotional, and professional well-being of professionals of color.

Despite the limitations the impediments place on a professional of color's career trajectory and workplace well-being, the authors recommended practical strategies to deal with the structural and psychological obstacles they face and how to flourish as a professional of color. Although there is not a panacea to resolve all issues that professionals of color will encounter in the workplace, some of the noted needs and strategies that we and the authors suggest to survive and thrive in higher education, especially at predominantly white institutions, include:

- Mentorship is truly needed to nurture your professional development, whether it occurs through formal, informal, or electronic means as well as cross-racial, cross-gender, or peer-to-peer.
- Professional support networks of peers, allies, and confidantes, as well as counterspaces, on and off campus, where you can construct and maintain yourself are necessary for equilibrium.
- A social network of family and friends is needed to provide social and emotional support to help mitigate any stressors and uplift you.
- Self-care is needed often, particularly putting yourself first when feeling overwhelmed while trying to balance competing demands of your time and attention. In addition, remember there is nothing wrong with asking for help, including seeking a professional counselor, when in need.
- Engage in self-love as often as possible and know your worth. Sometimes, you may need to set boundaries, protect yourself from toxic people and environments, focus more on what you need rather than want, and forgive yourself when needed. You may also need to remind yourself at times that you are not defined by your job and instead, define yourself by your beliefs, what you love to do, and who you love to be around.

- Self-discovery, self-reflection, and storytelling can be used to create context and legitimize your experiences, decisions, and pathways as well as to rejuvenate yourself.
- Know yourself and be authentic, which can hopefully encourage you to feel empowered, which can help you be the best version of yourself in all roles. "Try on" approaches you believe can work well for you in the work environment, but have an objective understanding of your personality, desires, motives, strengths, and weaknesses. Your actions should be in sync with your values while recognizing if you are instead just trying to please someone else or get something from someone.
- Determine which coping strategies, such as faith and spirituality, can be used as a guide and means to overcome stress and distress. Family and friends can sustain you during troubling times and encourage you whether they understand what you do or not.
- Build your social capital and professional repertoire as necessary for you to connect and grow. For example, learn all you can about your role and field, continue your education, take on new projects, participate in professional development, collaborate outside of your area, and diversify your experiences.
- Develop your transferable skills (e.g., communication, problem solving, planning, teamwork, and time management) to help you be adaptable in any role and marketable.
- Expand yourself, such as getting involved in consulting, publishing, researching, and conducting workshops and webinars, to be innovative and hone another set of skills.
- Learn the system, gain knowledge, and stay informed to help you in analyzing a situation or context and remaining vigilant. Be sure to also observe the politics in your work environment while learning to be politically savvy, which requires you to be socially astute, amicable, persuasive, credible, and sincere. In addition, evaluate what you have learned, and adapt as necessary.
- Avoid participation in divisiveness and "in-fighting" with other professionals of color. No one's light needs to be diminished or eliminated, believing there can be only one at the table, as everyone's light can shine simultaneously.
- Advocate for yourself, reach out, and connect to empower others.
- Recognize when it is time to move on and take your talents elsewhere. Of course, always do your homework first before going to a new institution or organization. Look for an environmental fit where you can contribute, thrive, and continue to grow.

The experiences of the authors can also be used to educate higher education administrators in positions of influence about the needs and barriers for professionals of color and highlight the need to address these issues and instigate change. Such complicated conversations are needed to shift the dynamics that thwart the effectiveness and accomplishments of professionals of color toward equitability and the conferral of opportunities based on merit and relevant and objective criteria. Of course, the communication of unconditional positive regard is a major curative factor in any approach to address the barriers and concerns professionals of color encounter, which consequently gives permission to the professional of color to have their own feelings, experiences, and realities. In the end, it is time for higher education to take a critical look at the experiences of professionals of color in student affairs and although progress does not always move in a straight line, it must happen. Certainly, it is worth critically appraising existing practices and approaches to honor the commitment to diversity espoused by institutions of higher education and implementing steady institutional support structures and policies developed through proactive, long-term planning. In the end, student affairs professionals of color are an undeniable asset to college environments and it is our hope that the narratives start a conversation that leads to action.

Above all, celebrate the small steps as well as the major accomplishments. Doing so can help you stay energized and positive.

ABOUT THE EDITORS

Dr. Monica Galloway Burke is an associate professor in the Department of Counseling and Student Affairs at Western Kentucky University. She earned a Bachelor of Arts degree in psychology from Tougaloo College; a Master of Science degree in counseling psychology from the University of Southern Mississippi; and a Doctor of Philosophy degree in educational administration and supervision with an emphasis in higher education from the University of Southern Mississippi. Prior to her 21 years of experience as a faculty member and practitioner in student affairs and higher education, she worked in the field of mental health.

Dr. Burke's research interests include college student development; professional development; helping and coping skills; and topics related to diversity and societal issues. She has authored numerous peer-reviewed articles in scholarly journals and contributed chapters to various books. Furthermore, she served as the lead author for *Helping Skills for Working With College Students: Applying Counseling Theory to Student Affairs Practice* (Routledge, 2017) and is a co-editor for *No Ways Tired: The Journey for Professionals of Color in Student Affairs.* She also serves as a co-editor for two upcoming books related to higher education professionals working with college students in distress. Additionally, Dr. Burke has conducted over 100 workshops and presentations at the international, national, regional, state, and local levels.

Dr. Burke currently serves and has served on editorial boards of professional journals as a co-editor, associate editor, and reviewer. She also supervised numerous research theses, dissertations, and research projects, some of which led to co-authored published manuscripts with students. Dr. Burke

No Ways Tired, pages 155–156

remains actively involved in professional associations and has consistently held leadership roles in the Southern Association for College Student Affairs (SACSA). In addition, she is committed to service within the campus and local community. Dr. Burke has received recognition and several awards for her commitment to preparing graduate students for a career in student affairs, her efforts and scholarship to promote the field of student affairs, and her work related to diversity in higher education.

Dr. U. Monique Robinson is the assistant dean for Peabody College student affairs at Vanderbilt University, where she is responsible for undergraduate, professional, and online students. She provides undergraduate academic support and is the liaison to campus mental health and wellness resources. Additionally, she oversees various aspects of orientation, retention, and commencement. Prior to Vanderbilt University, she was the director of student life and diversity initiatives at Volunteer State Community College (VSCC) in Gallatin, Tennessee. Now with 28 years in higher education, she began her career as assistant director of Admissions at Nazareth College.

Her educational background includes a Bachelor of Science in studio art from Nazareth College. Monique has a Masters of Education in student personnel services and Doctor of Education in higher education administration, both from Peabody College at Vanderbilt University.

Dr. Robinson, who has been actively engaged in community service, especially related to mentoring, is a member and past officer of the Nashville Metropolitan Alumnae Chapter of Delta Sigma Theta Sorority, Inc. and past local chapter president and national secretary of Societas Docta, Inc. She has volunteered with the NAACP ACT-SO program, served several terms on the National Conference on Race and Ethnicity (NCORE) National Advisory Committee and currently, serves on the board of R.A.C.E. Mentoring. She received VSCC's Outstanding Professional/Administrative Award, the Women in Higher Education in Tennessee (WHET) June Anderson Award, the Association for the Promotion of Campus Activities Leadership Award, and Peabody College's Distinguished College Staff Award, and is a graduate of Vanderbilt Leadership Academy. Most recently, she received the Organization of Black Graduate and Professional Student Distinguished Faculty Award.

ABOUT THE CONTRIBUTORS

Aliya Beavers is the director of the Office of Student Diversity, Equity, and Inclusion at the University of Houston-Clear Lake. She is also a doctoral student in the Higher, Adult, and Lifelong Education PhD program at Michigan State University. During her 10+ years in various student affairs roles, Aliya has been able to explore one of her research passions, the experiences of multicultural persons in higher education.

Ginny Jones Boss, PhD, is an assistant professor of leadership studies at Kennesaw State University. Ginny has been in the field of student affairs for 10 years and worked in residence life prior to joining faculty full time.

Harold Brown currently serves as a program coordinator in the Office of Greek Life at Vanderbilt University. Harold holds 5 years of student affairs experience with collective skills in fraternity and sorority life, career development, and diversity and inclusion. He is a second year doctoral student at Tennessee State University in the EdD program for educational leadership.

Hoa Bui, MS, is currently an area coordinator in Residence Life and Community Development at La Salle University. Bui's journey in student affairs started with her involvement in activism at Colgate University, her alma mater. She subsequently served as a resident director at Miami University. Passionate about decoloniality, transnational feminism, and international education, Bui has published a few book chapters and journal articles on these topics.

No Ways Tired, pages 157–160
Copyright © 2019 by Information Age Publishing
157

Karla Cruze-Silva is a scholar-practitioner who is currently a doctoral student in the Center for the Study of Higher Education at the University of Arizona. Karla currently serves as the manager for wellness initiatives at the University of Arizona. Her passions within higher education include serving students who are first generation, have a high financial need, and previous research includes understanding the PhD pipeline for Latinx students.

Roberto Cruze is a scholar-practitioner who received his master's in student affairs in higher education from Colorado State University. Roberto currently serves students as the program coordinator for the TRiO Student Support Services Project GReAT Program at Pima Community College. Roberto's work towards the advancement of Latina/o/x students and professionals to and through higher education by utilizing scholarship as means of informing practice and the utilizing practice as a means of informing scholarship.

Janessa J. Dunn, MEd, is an assistant director of admissions in the Office of Undergraduate Admissions at Vanderbilt University. She has lead recruitment and yield programs grounded in access, affordability, and inclusion at Vanderbilt University for 3 years. She is also a member of the National Association of College Admissions Counseling (NACAC), a member of affiliate NACAC organizations in the Midwest region, and a volunteer for college access programs in her local community.

Jarett D. Haley is a PhD student in the Center for the Study of Higher and Postsecondary Education at the University of Michigan. Prior to beginning his graduate studies, he spent 3 years at Swarthmore College working in Career Services.

Terrance Harris, MEd, is the director of the Lonnie B. Harris Black Cultural Center (in the Office of Diversity and Cultural Engagement) at Oregon State University. Terrance has been in the field of student affairs for 7 years. He is a member of a plethora of professional organizations and community groups.

Tassany C. Henderson, EdD, is a program coordinator in the Dean of Students office at Vanderbilt University in Nashville, TN. Tassany has been in the field of student affairs for 6 years and serves as a TN Promise mentor within the Nashville community. She serves on several committees within the higher education industry and is currently the 2nd vice president of Women in Higher Education of Tennessee.

Carol Huang, MA, is a career counselor/coordinator in career services at the University of California, Santa Barbara. Carol's student affairs work has been driven by her strong desire to understand and impact individuals and communities by connecting their passions with purpose and creating opportunities to achieve their goals. Her interests include career and leadership development, working with first-generation college students and students of color, the experiences of Asian Pacific Americans in higher education, and women of color professional development.

Brooke Huynh is in her last year of the college student personnel program in the Human Development and Family Studies Department at the University of Rhode Island. Her journey into student affairs began at Hampshire College, where she worked in the Campus Leadership and Activities Office. She is also a vice chair of the ACPA Commission for Social Justice Education and she is a strong advocate for social justice and anti-racism pedagogy in higher education.

Nadeeka Karunaratne, MA, is a doctoral student in the higher education and organizational change program at the University of California, Los Angeles. She has worked in multiple student affairs functional areas, including academic support services, multicultural affairs, and sexual violence prevention.

Jasmine Kelly is an educational program specialist at Georgia State University. She has been in the field for 2 years and is also a second-year doctoral student in the higher education leadership program at Clark Atlanta University.

Vigor Lam, MEd, is a project engineer II at Kitchell CEM, working with the City College of San Francisco on their facilities master plan. Prior to this role, he worked in higher education for 5 years in various functional areas including campus and student activities, campus life, residential life, and academic affairs. He is an active member of a few professional and nonprofit higher education, Asian American advocacy, and construction management organizations.

Gary Santos Mendoza, MSEd, is a PhD student in the educational leadership and research methodology program at Florida Atlantic University (FAU) whose research explores Queer Latinx students' experiences in Queer Centers. Gary served as assistant director for the Office of Campus Life–Broward, Diversity and Multicultural Affairs, and teaches undergraduate leadership courses at FAU. He is a member of ACPA—College Student Educators International and is involved with the Coalition for Gender and Sexual Identities and the Latinx Network.

Diana Morris, MEd, is an assistant director in the Office of Student Accountability, Community Standards, and Academic Integrity at Vanderbilt University. Diana has been in the field of student affairs for 6 years and has held positions in international education, housing and residence life, and student conduct. Outside of her work in student affairs, Diana is also a writer and personal development coach.

Catherine Ramírez, MEd, is a senior academic advisor in the Office of Admissions and Academic Advising for the College of Arts and Sciences at Cornell University. She has been in the field for over three years and has had experiences in various roles within the field.

Joi Sampson, MS, is the associate director of career and professional development at Mercy College. She is interested in equitable access to education for underrepresented populations and has worked to bring awareness of issues pertaining to higher education on Capitol Hill. She is currently pursuing a doctorate in higher education leadership at Manhattanville College.

Marcus Scales, MEd, is the assistant director of residence life at Widener University. Marcus has been in the field of student affairs for 8 years.

Charlie A. Scott is a Diné (Navajo) scholar from the central part of the Navajo Nation. They recieved their MS from The University of Rhode Island and will be a doctoral student in higher education at the University of Denver starting Fall 2019.

Thaddeus Stegall, MA, previously served as a residential college director in residential education and currently serves as associate instructor of music and producer at New York University Abu Dhabi (NYUAD). Thaddeus is an entry-level professional who has worked extensively with gifted students, international students, and students of color, in three different countries.

Kevin L. Wright, MA, is the Black/African American program coordinator in the Office of Student Diversity and Social Justice at the University of Nevada, Las Vegas. Kevin has been in the field of student affairs for 5 years and is also pursuing a Doctor of Education in professional leadership, inquiry, and transformation. He previously earned his bachelor's degree from Northern Arizona University and master's degree from Lewis & Clark College.